May this book be more than just a pastime; let it be a portal to moments of tranquility, where stress disappears and joy takes shape through colors.

Awaken the artist within you and let yourself be enveloped by the magic of "Magic Animal Mandalas to Color and Relax".

The adventure is about to begin.

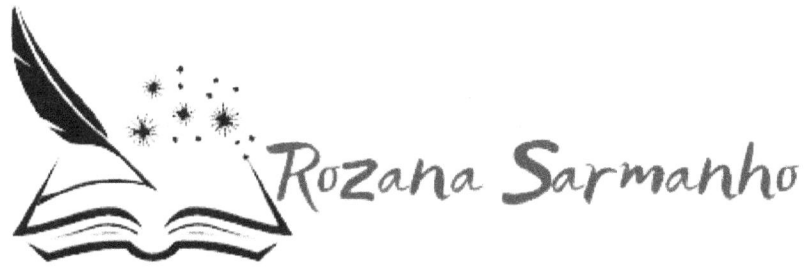

Test Color Page

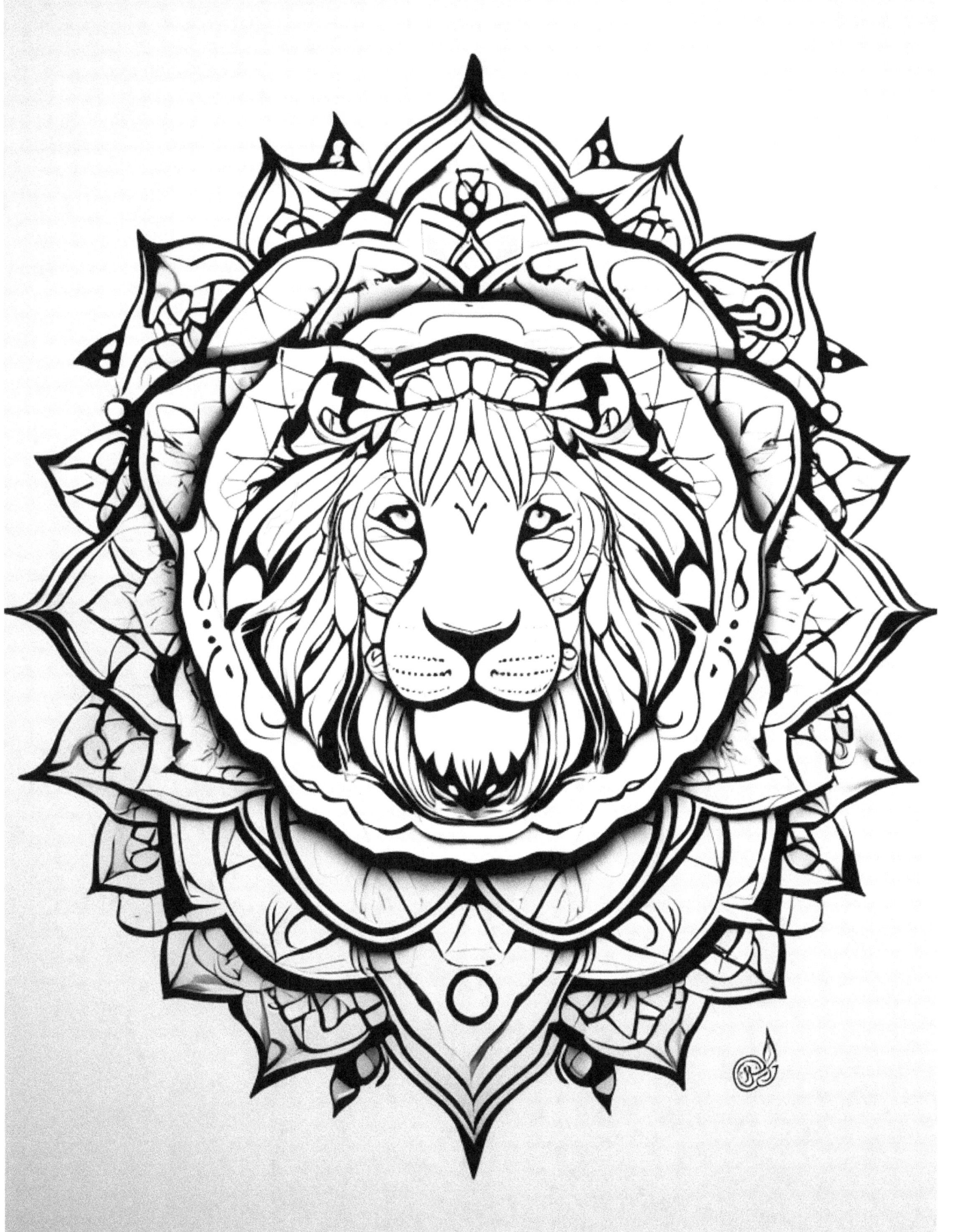

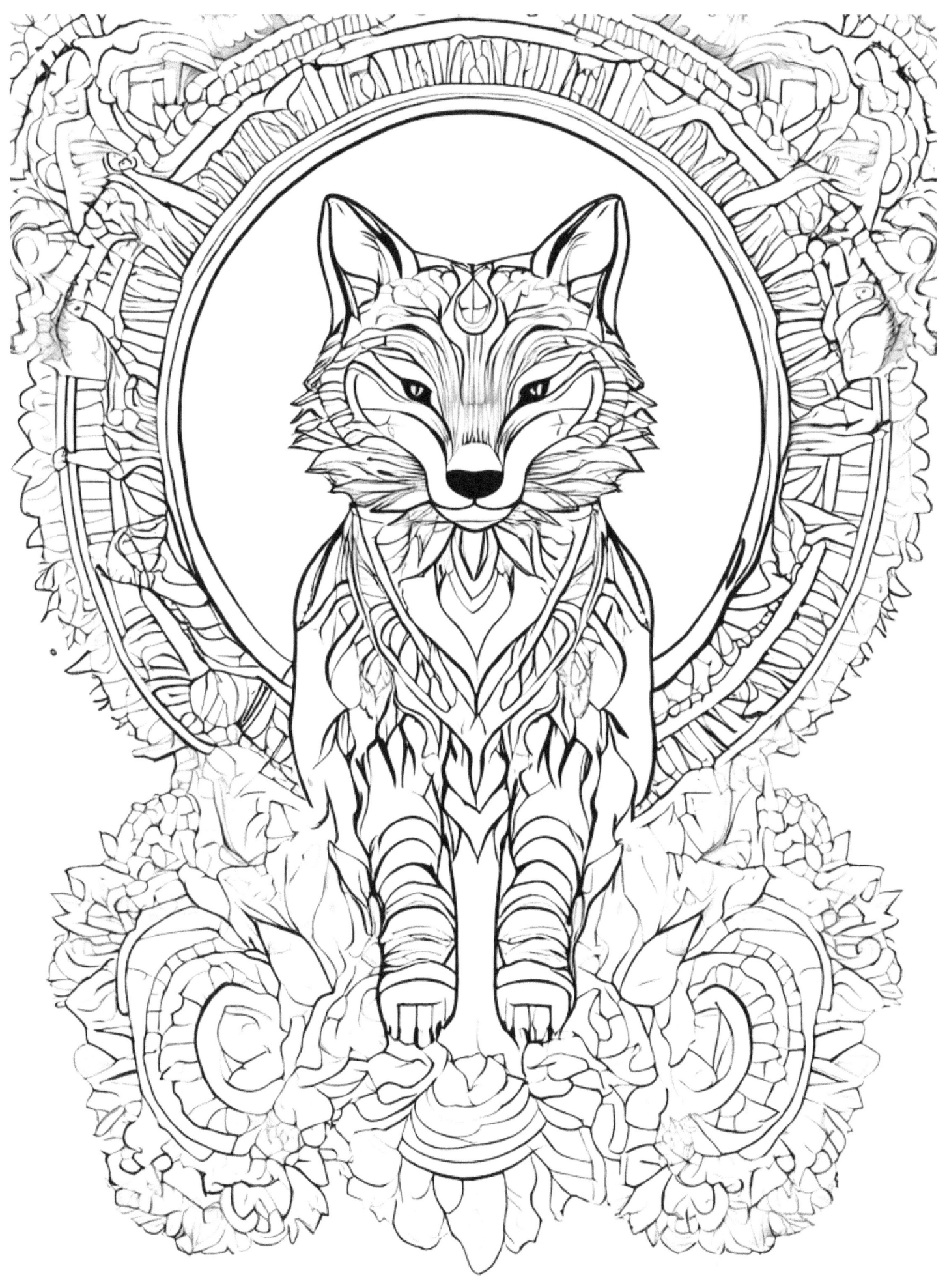

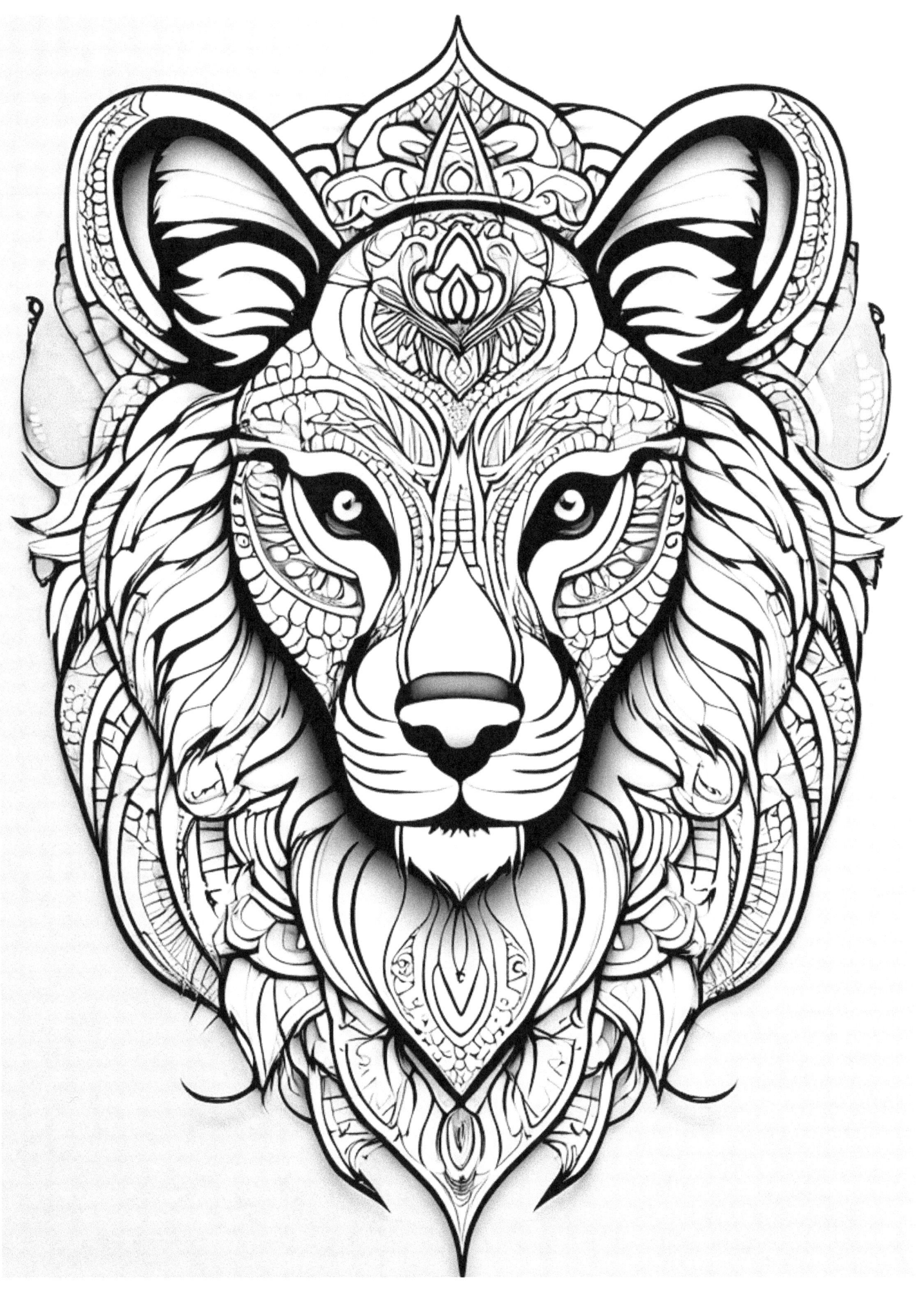

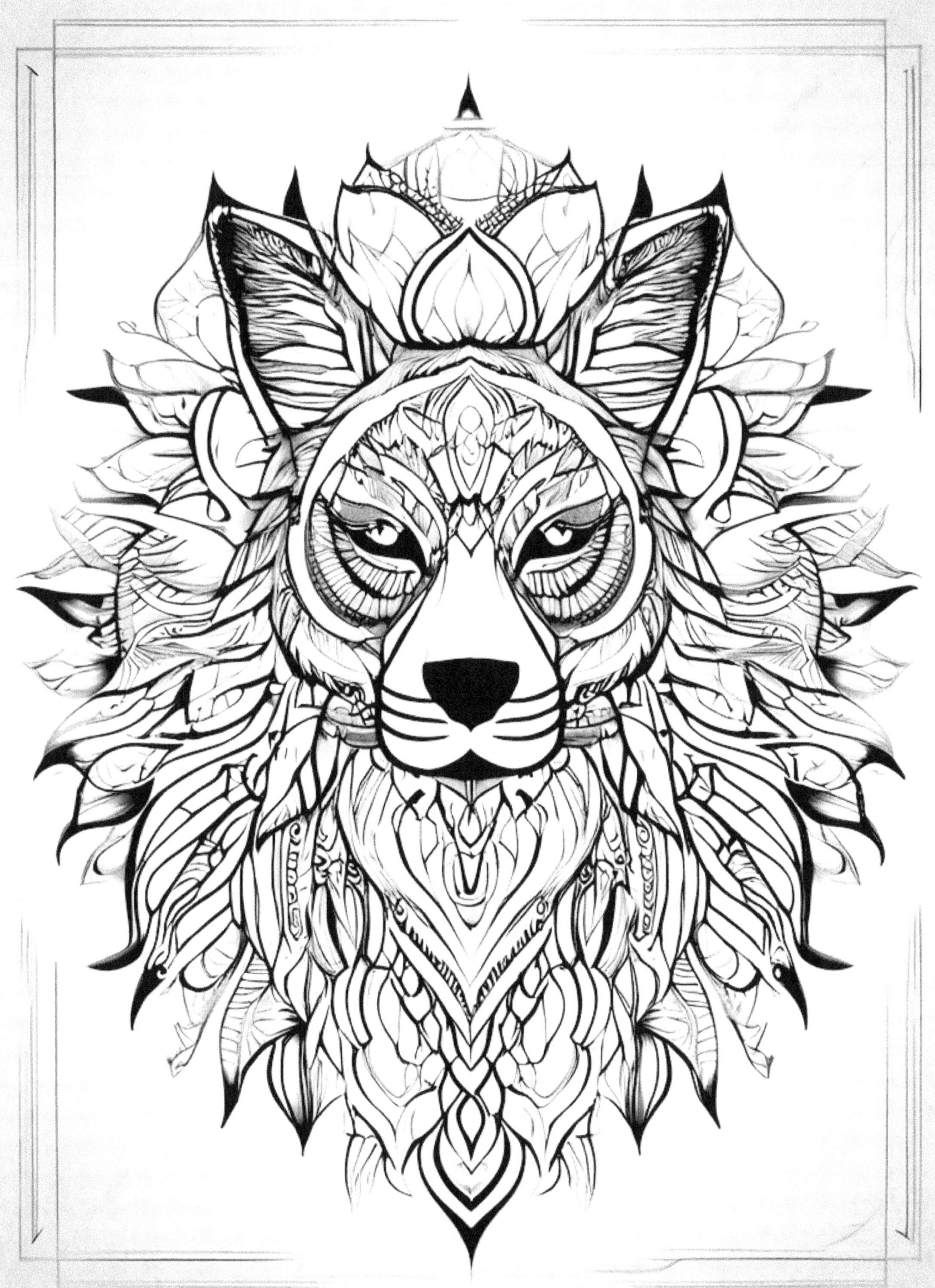

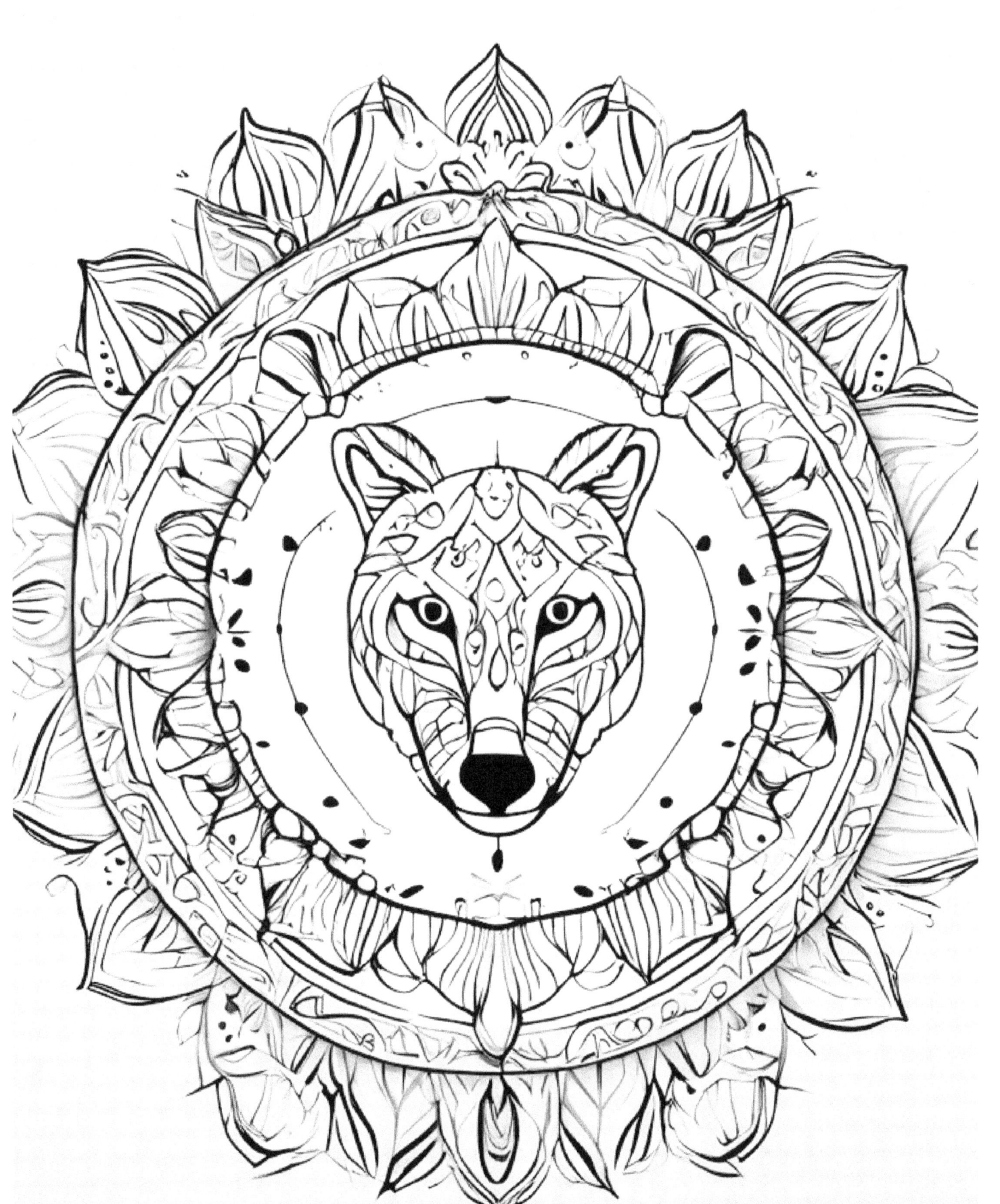

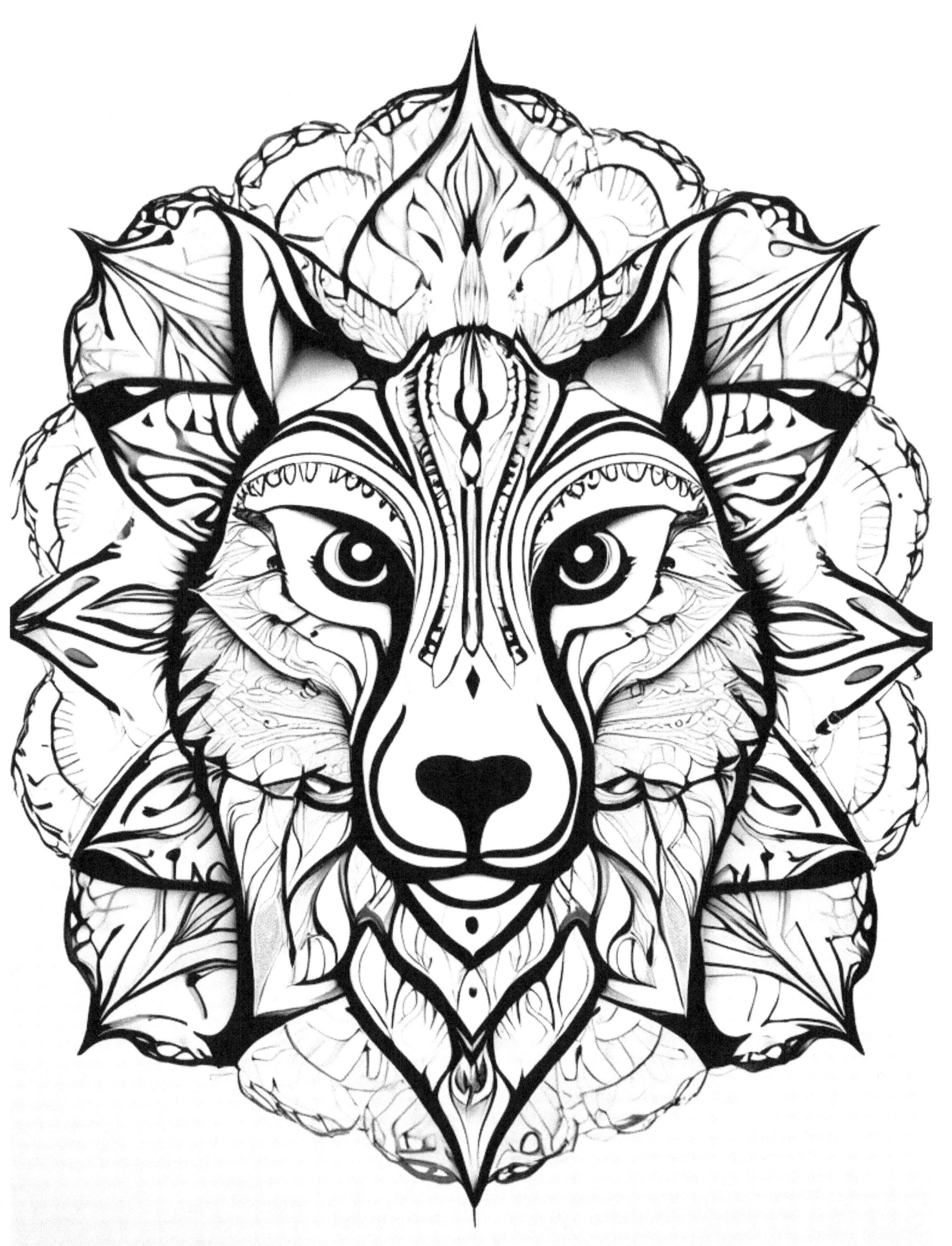

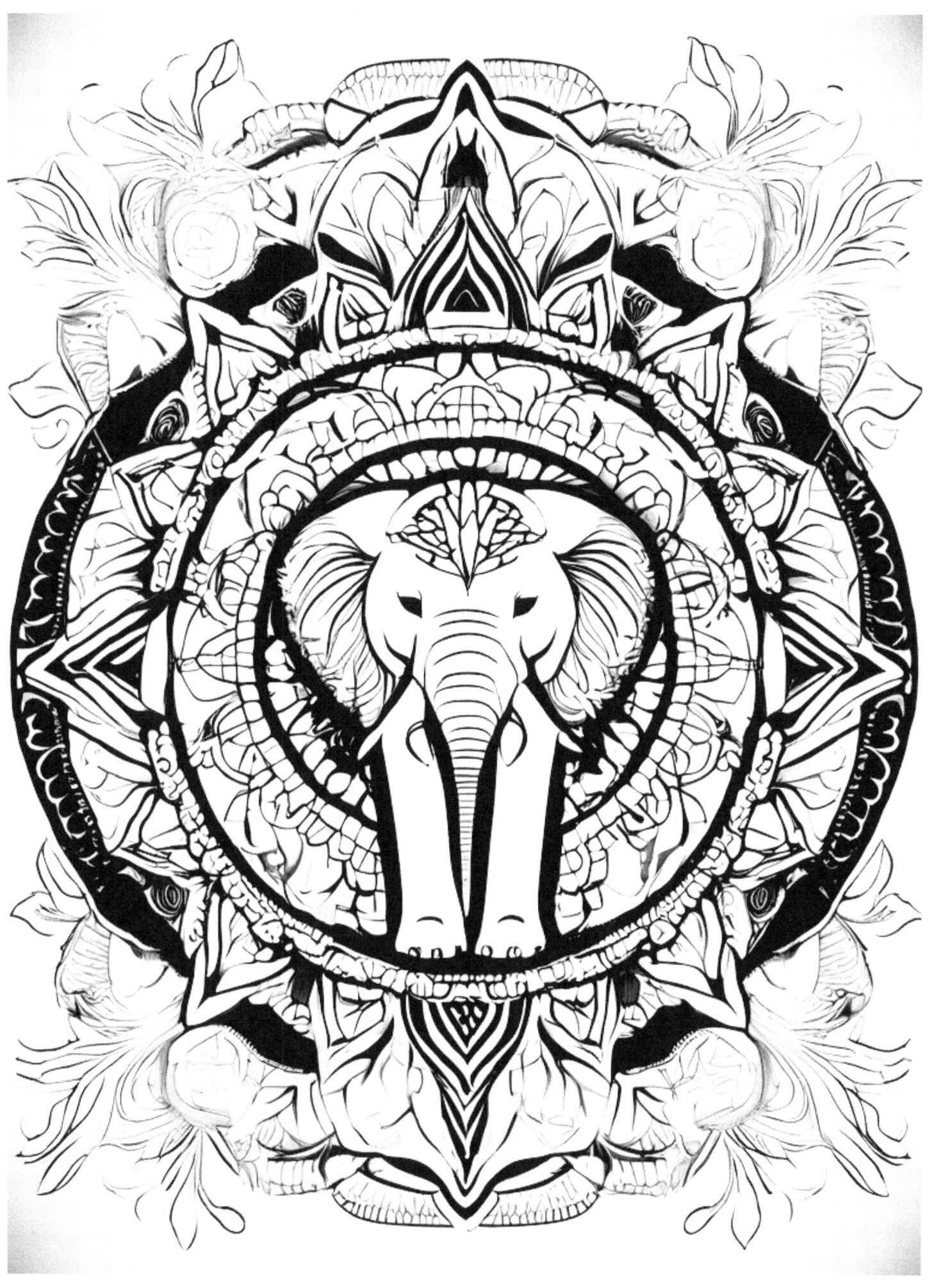

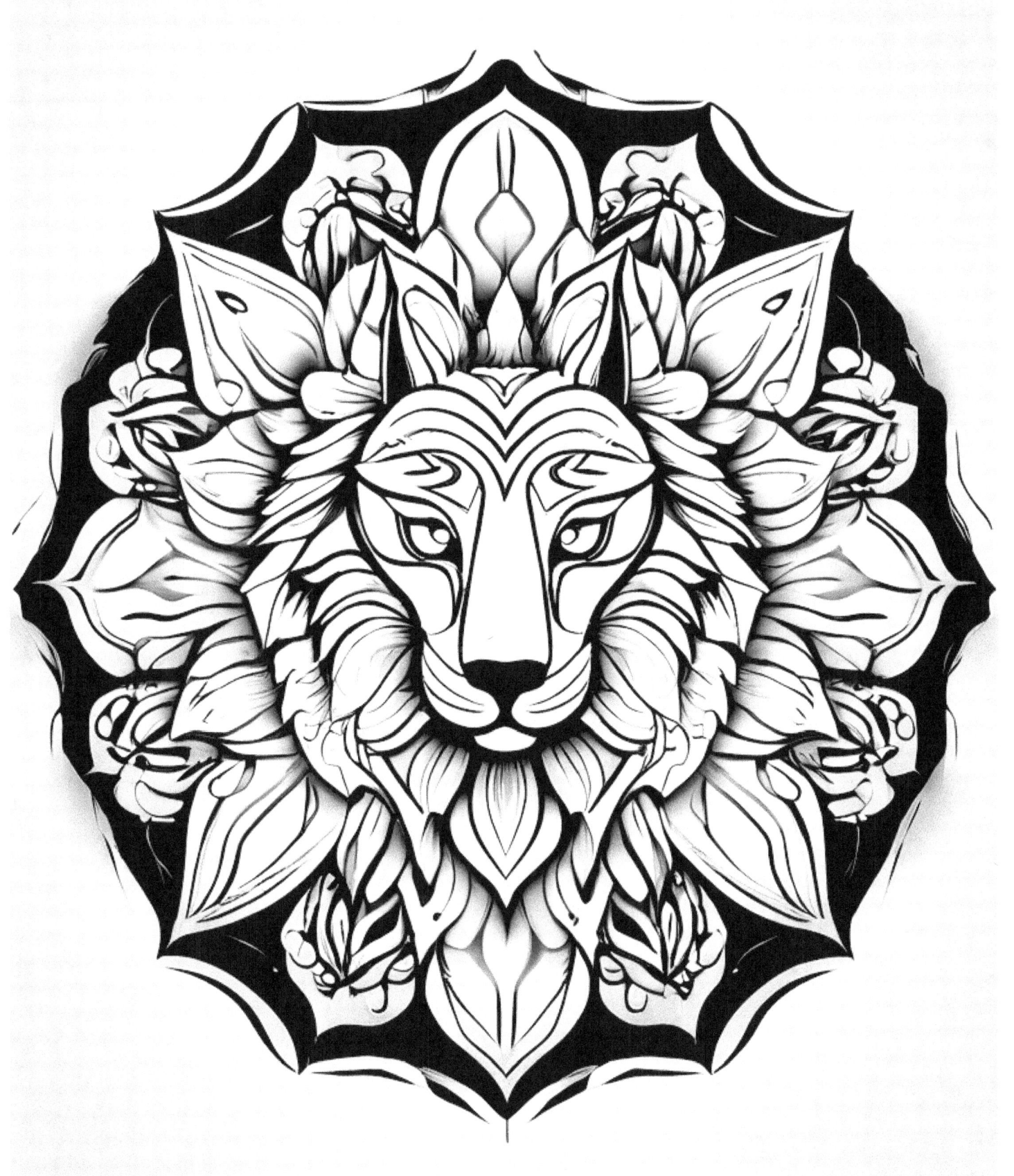

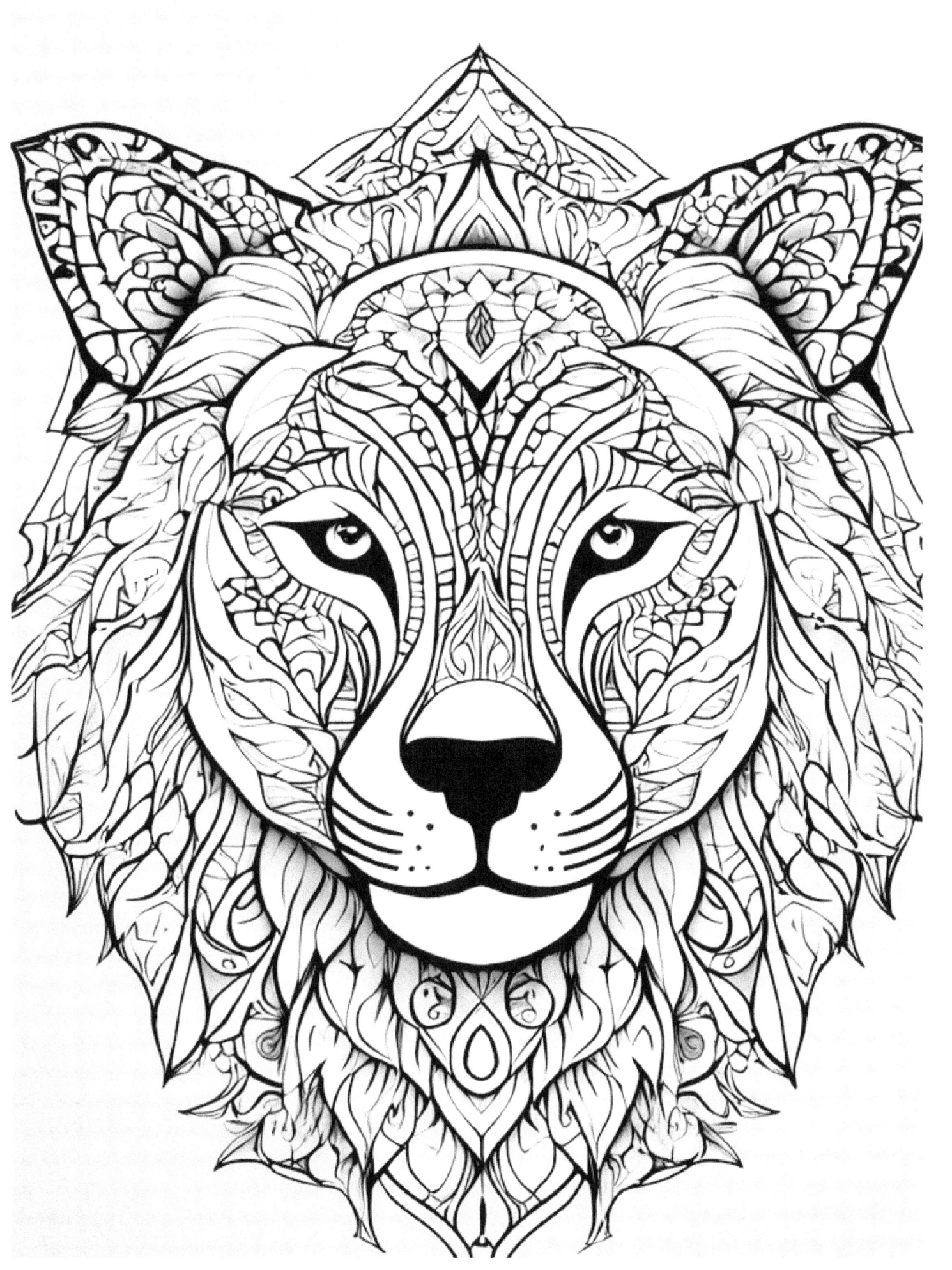

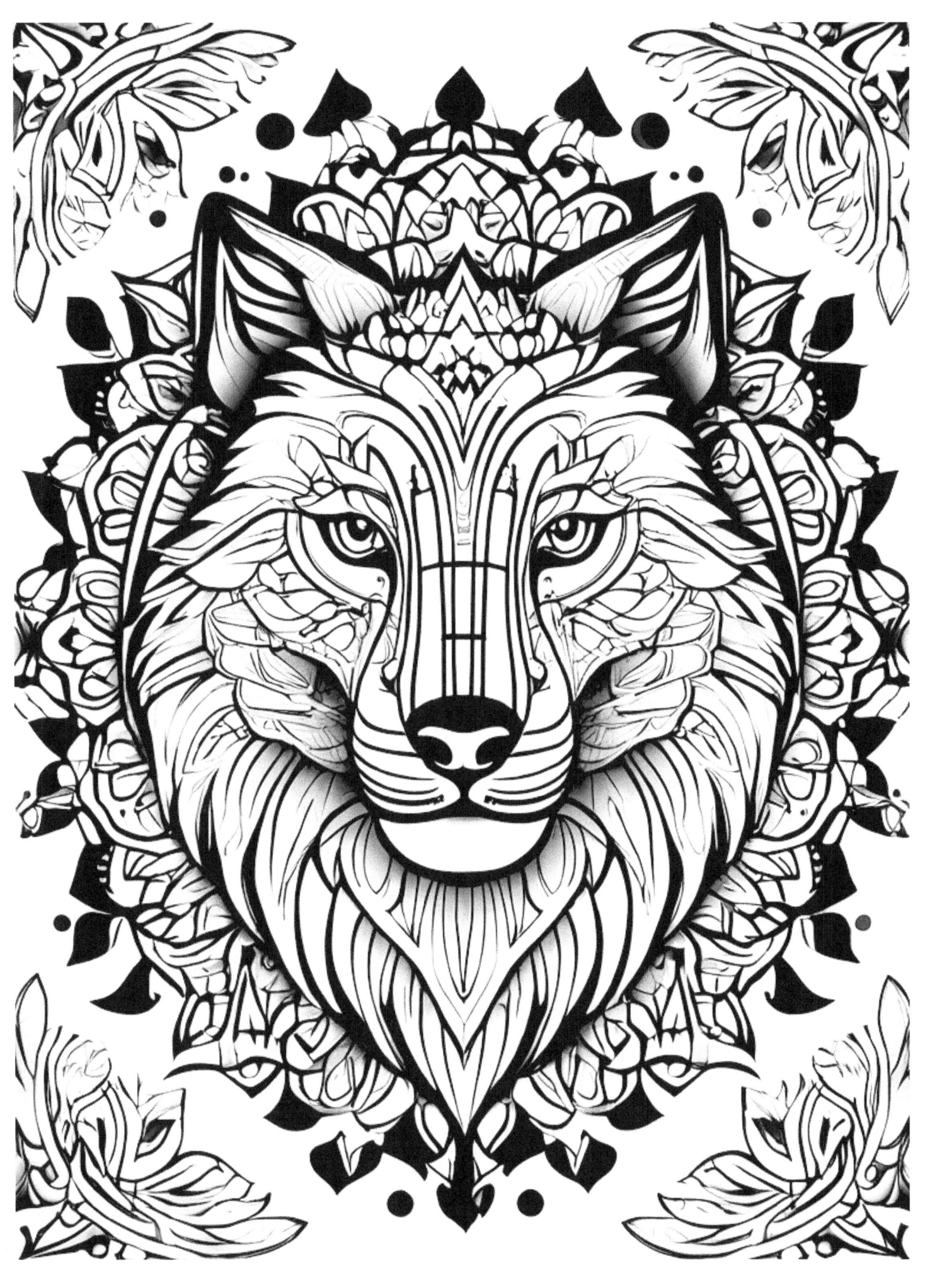

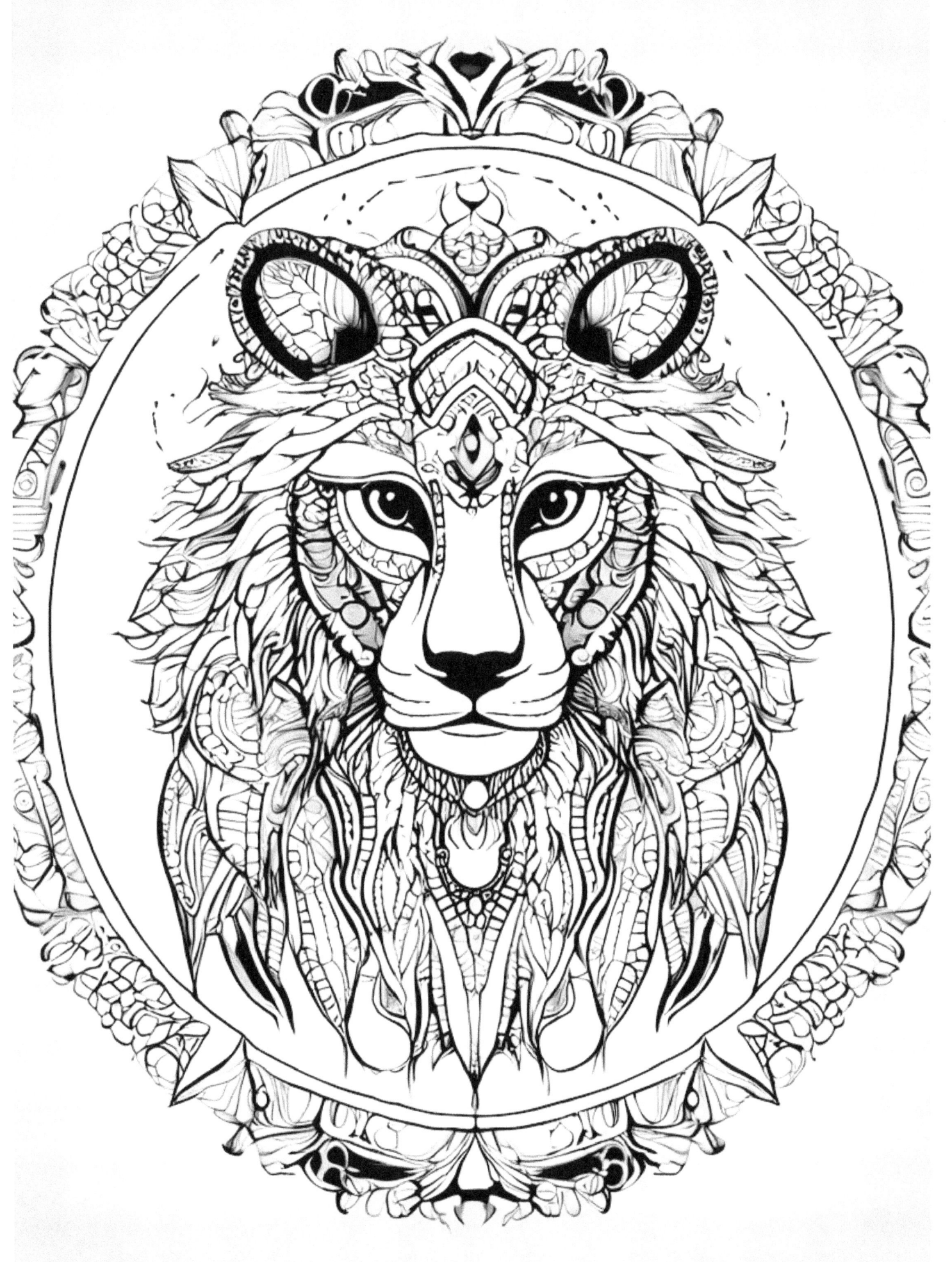

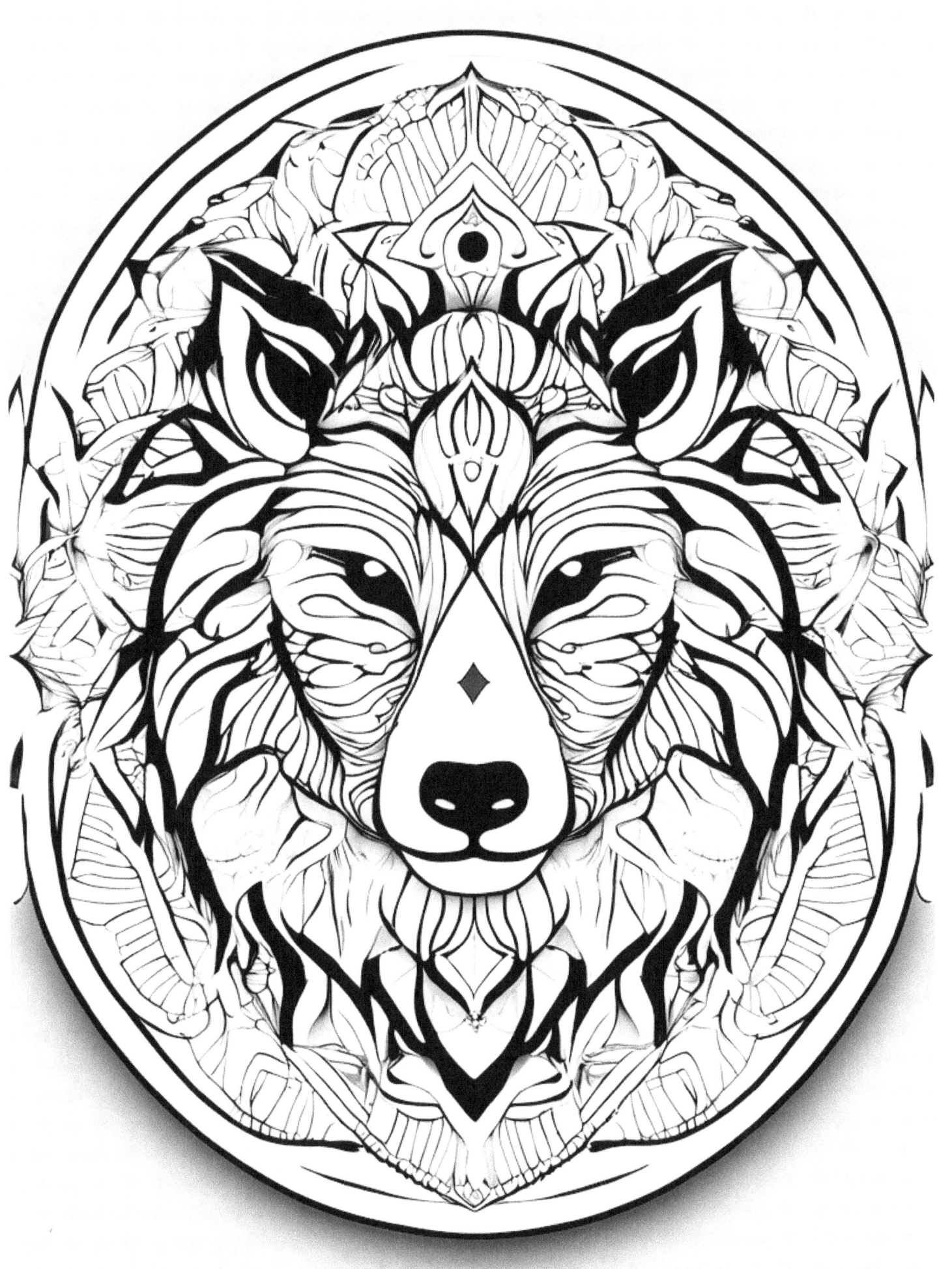

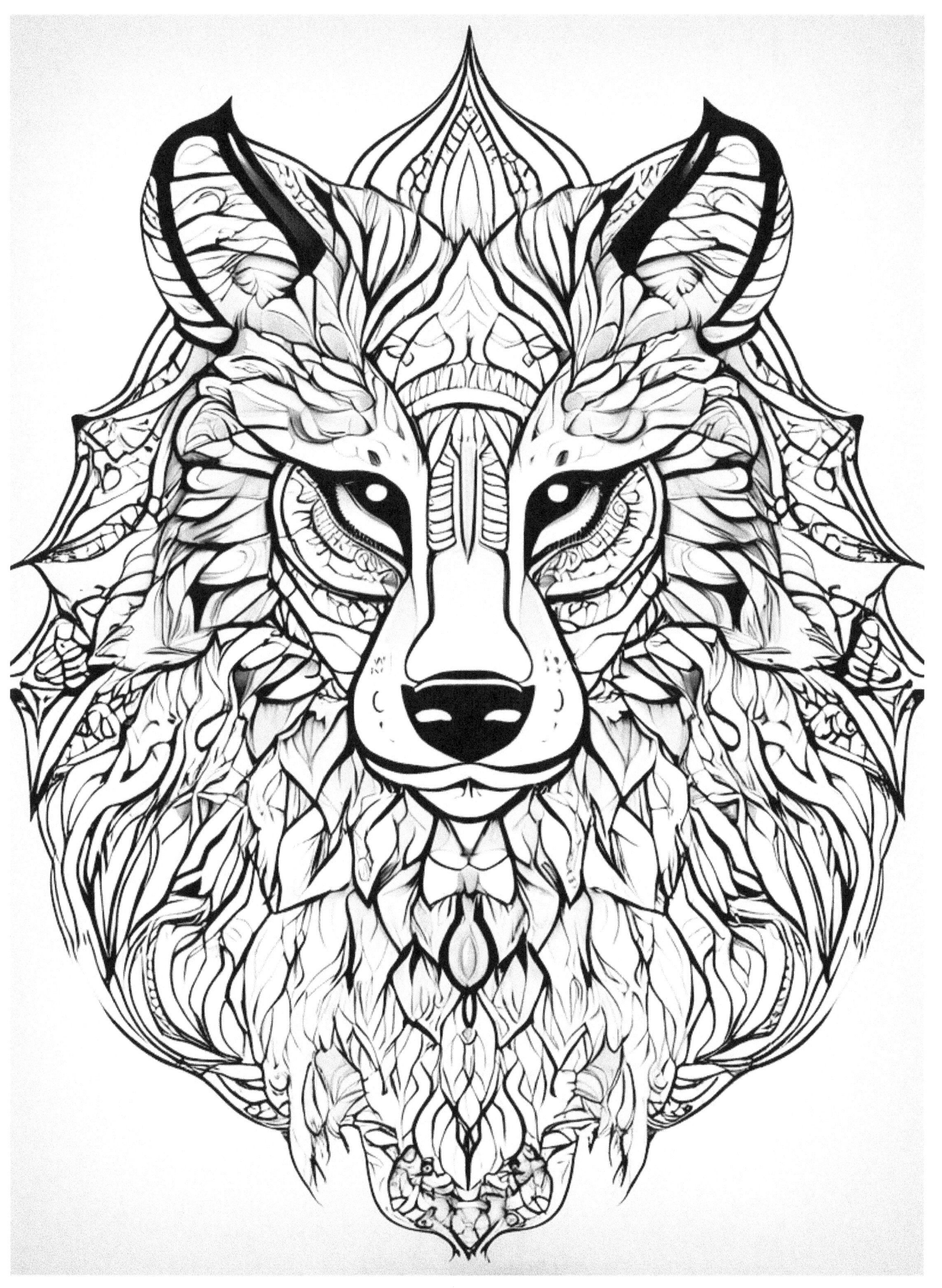

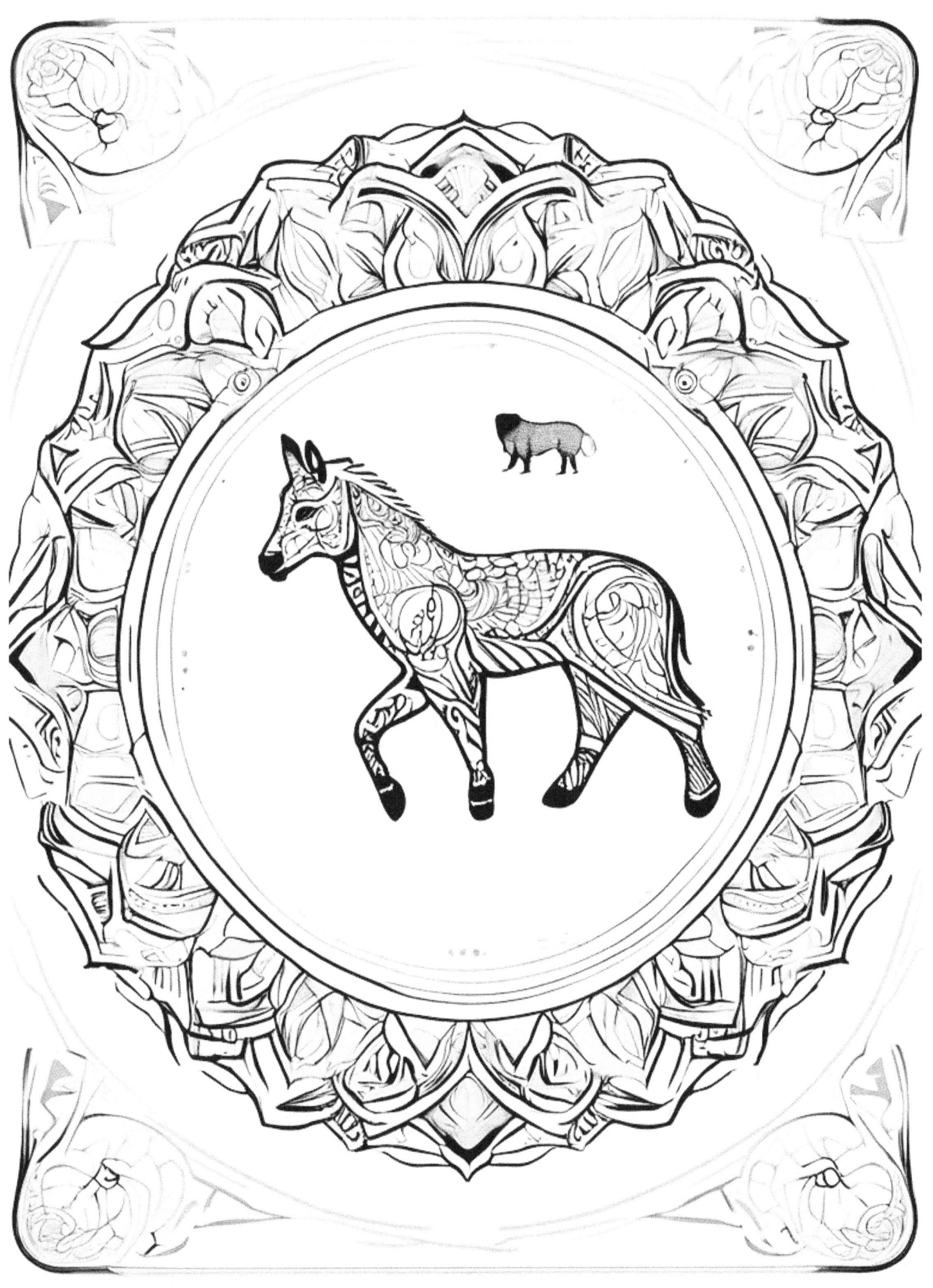

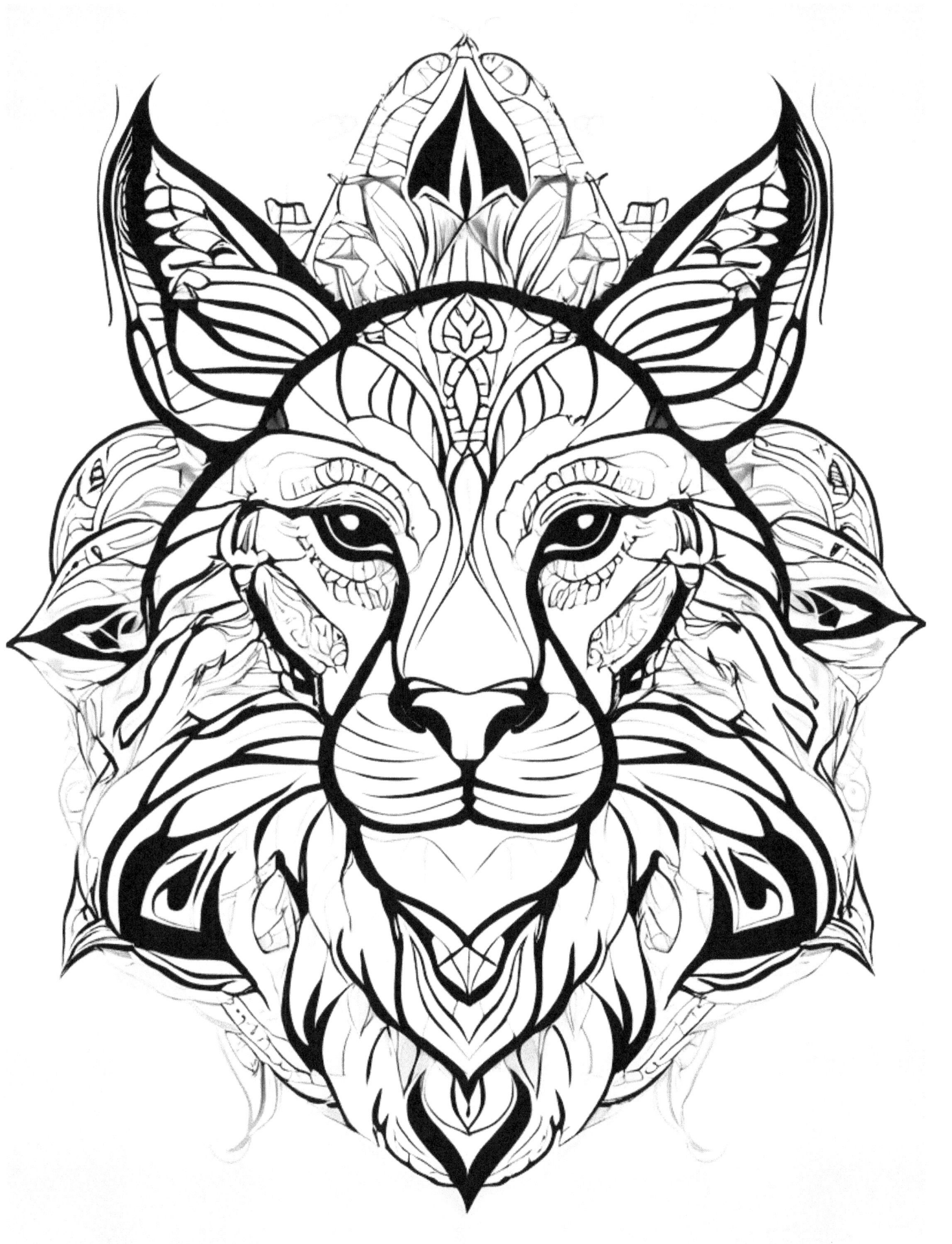

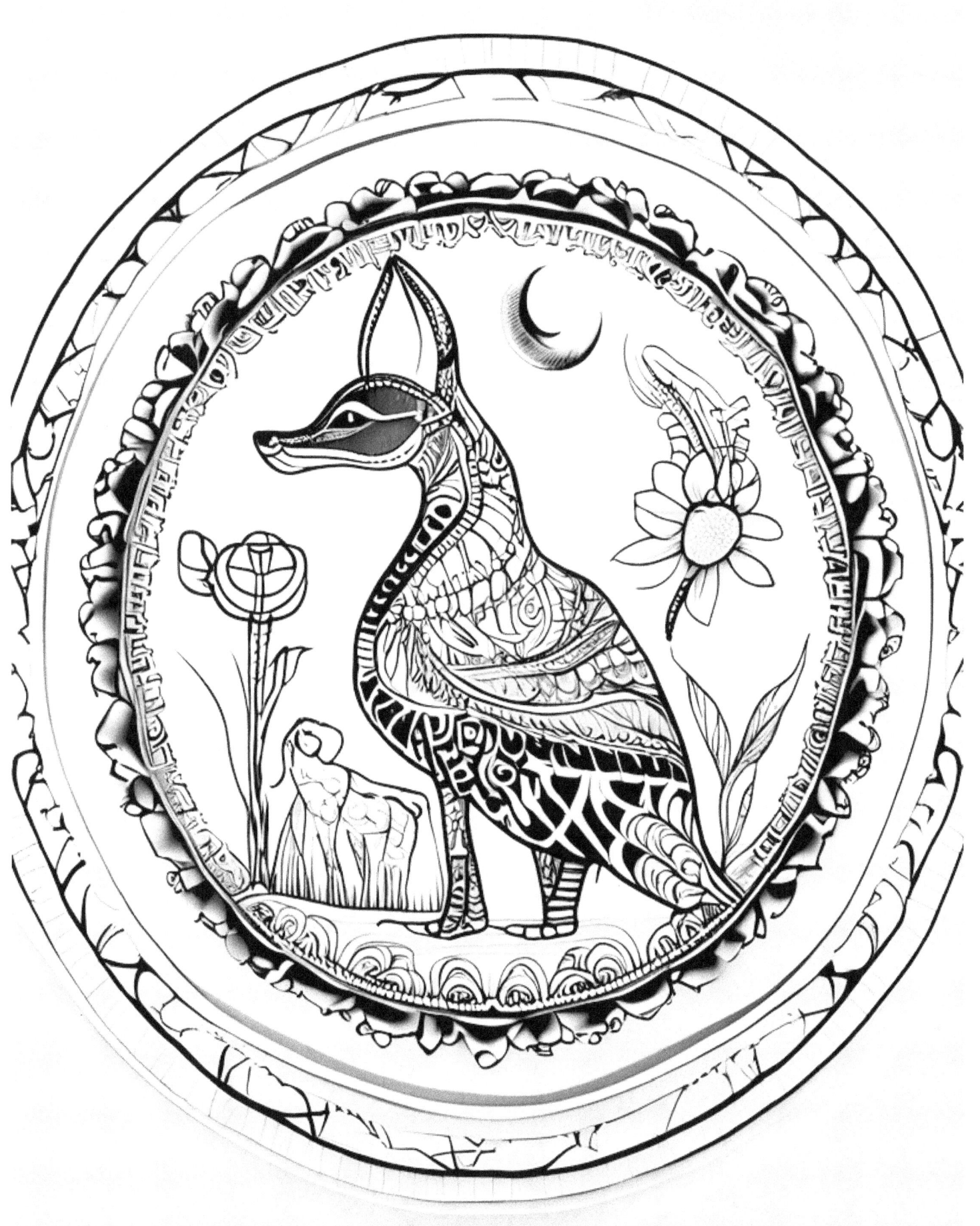

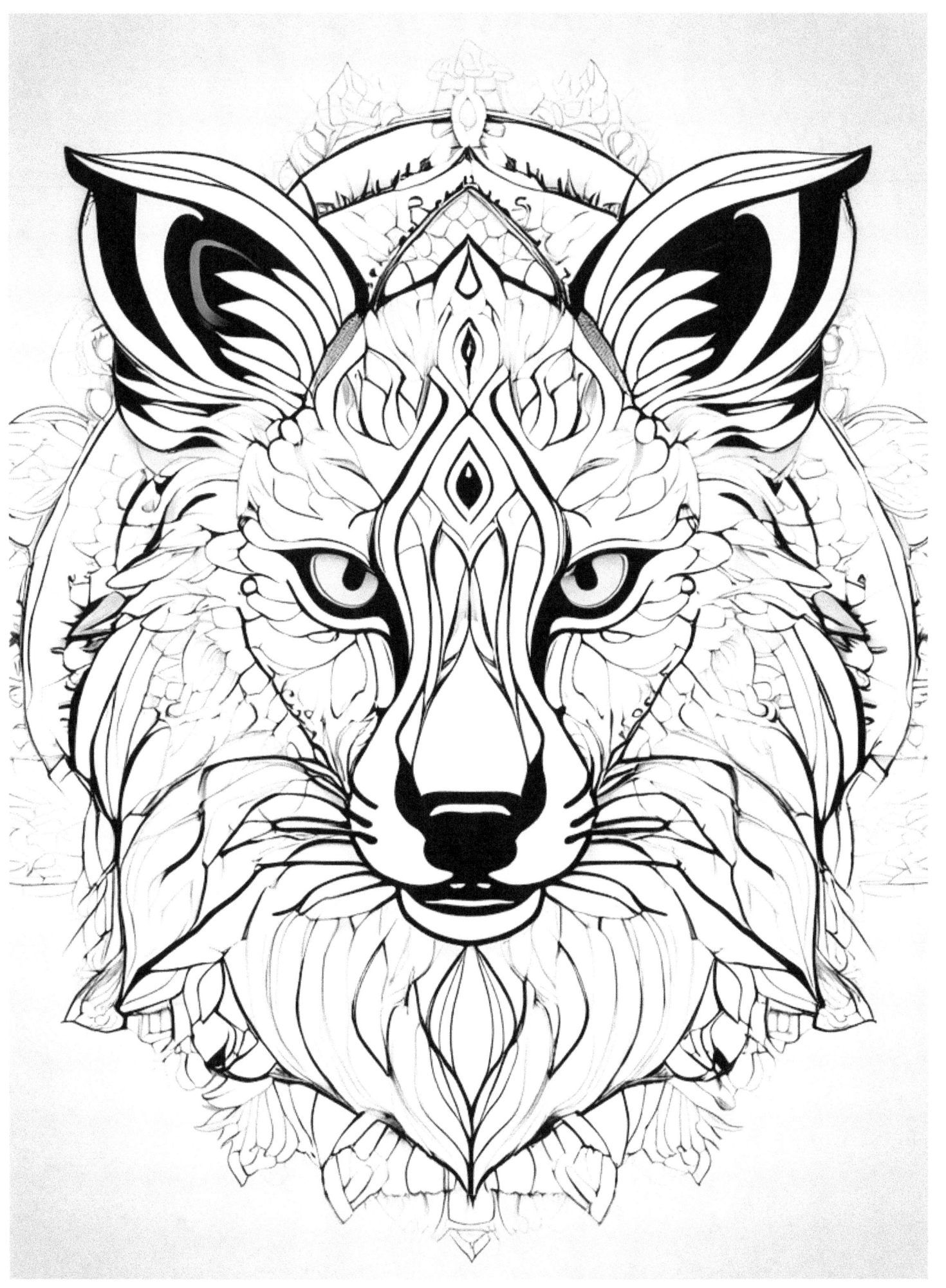

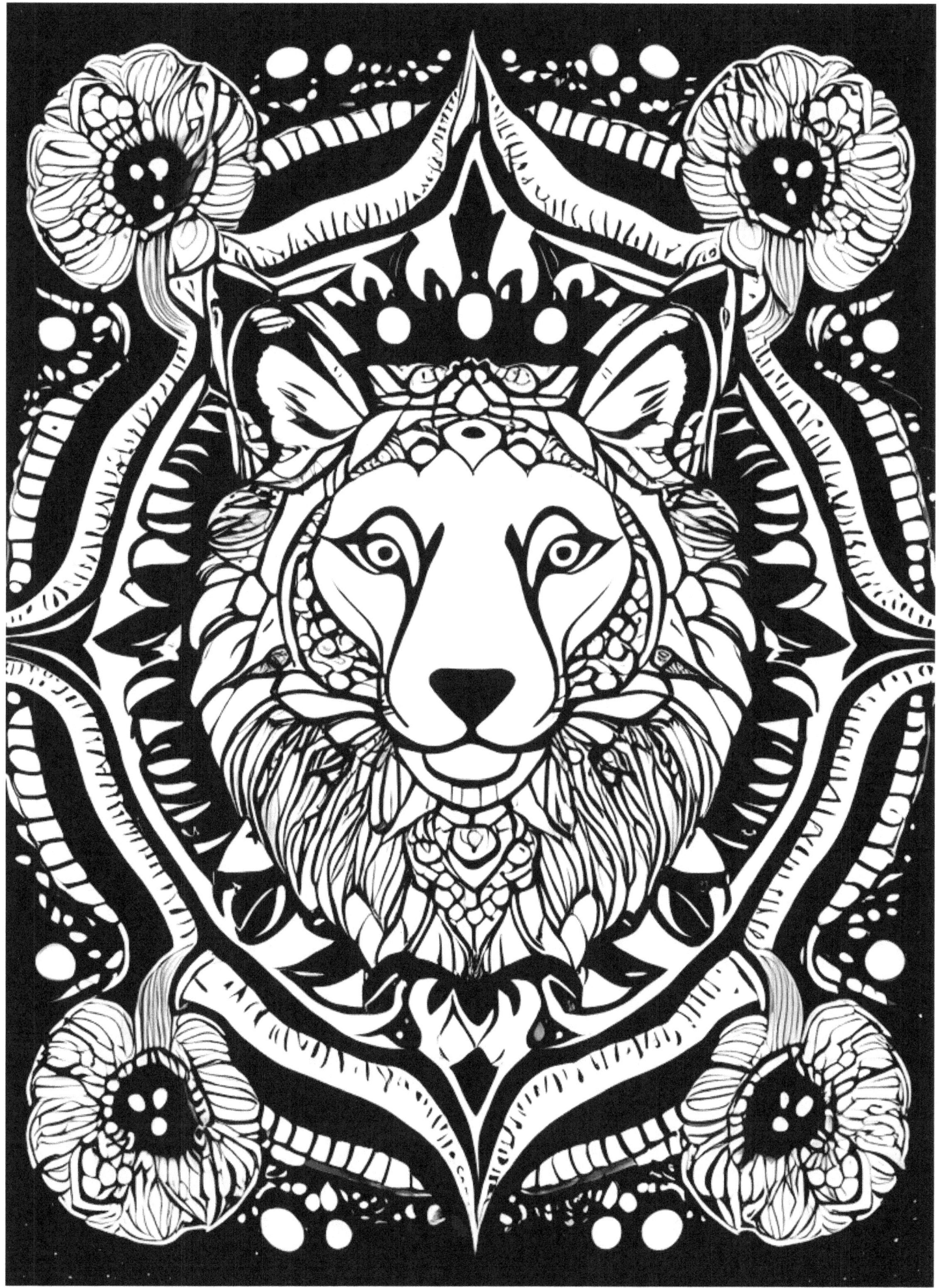

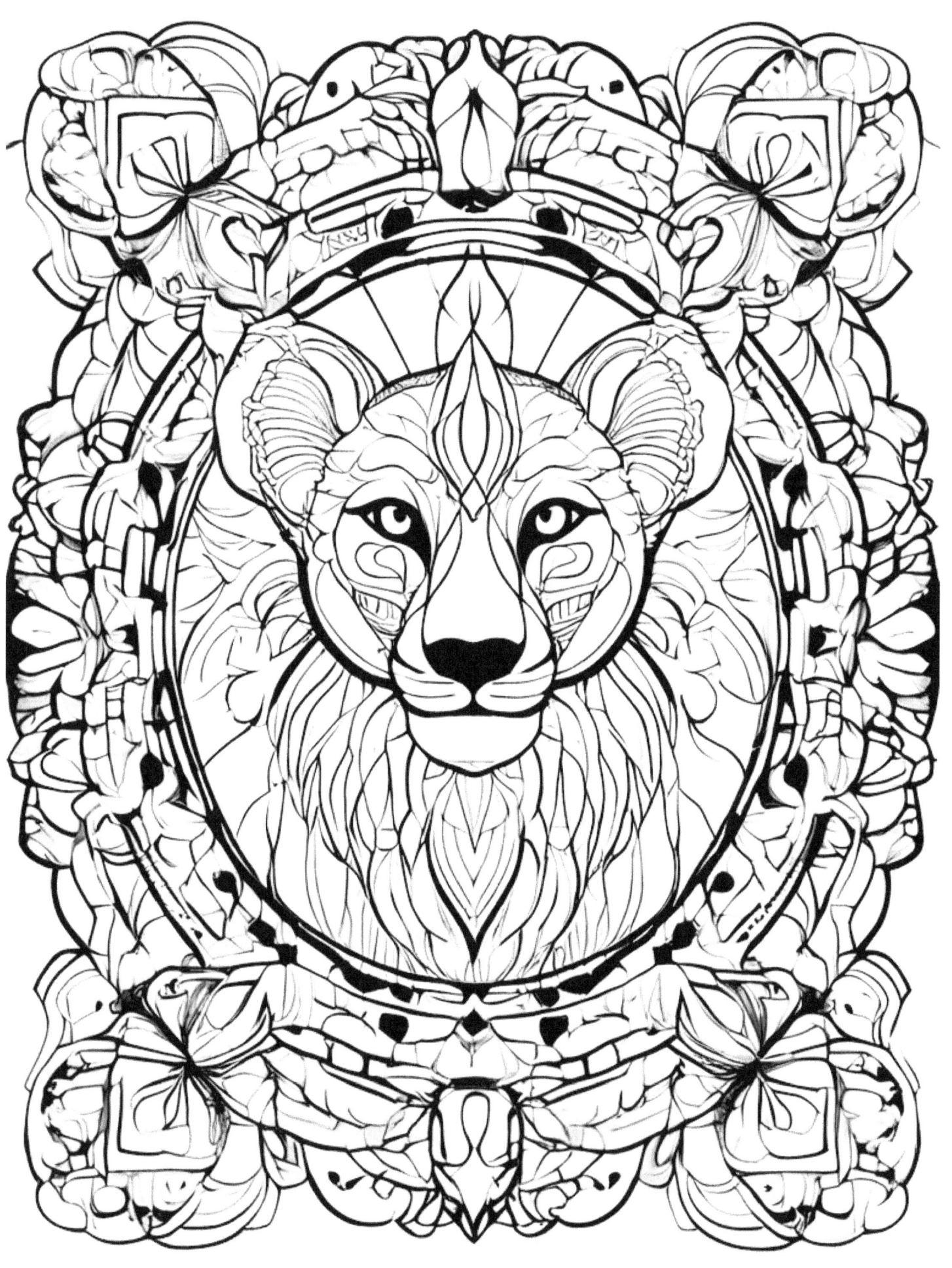

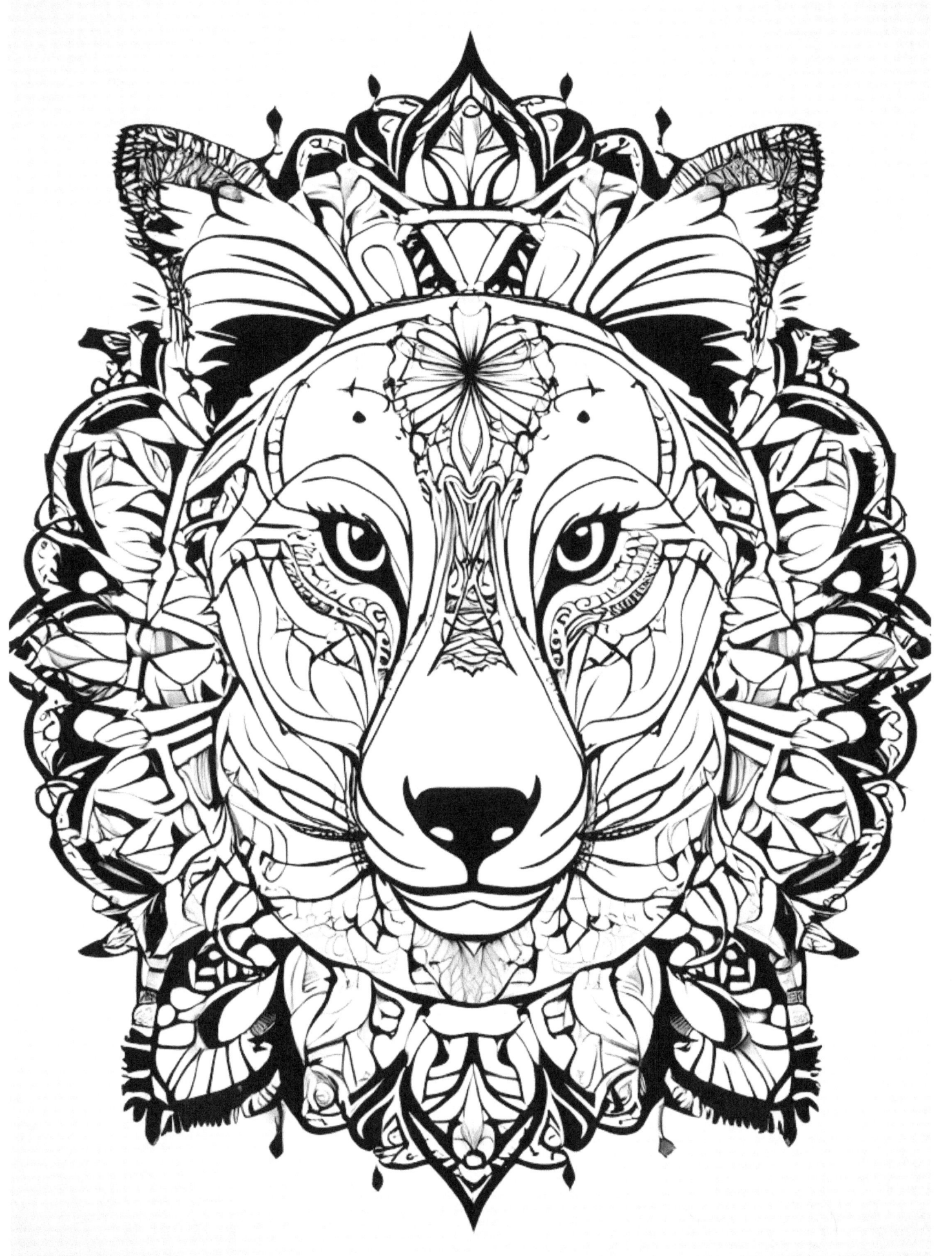

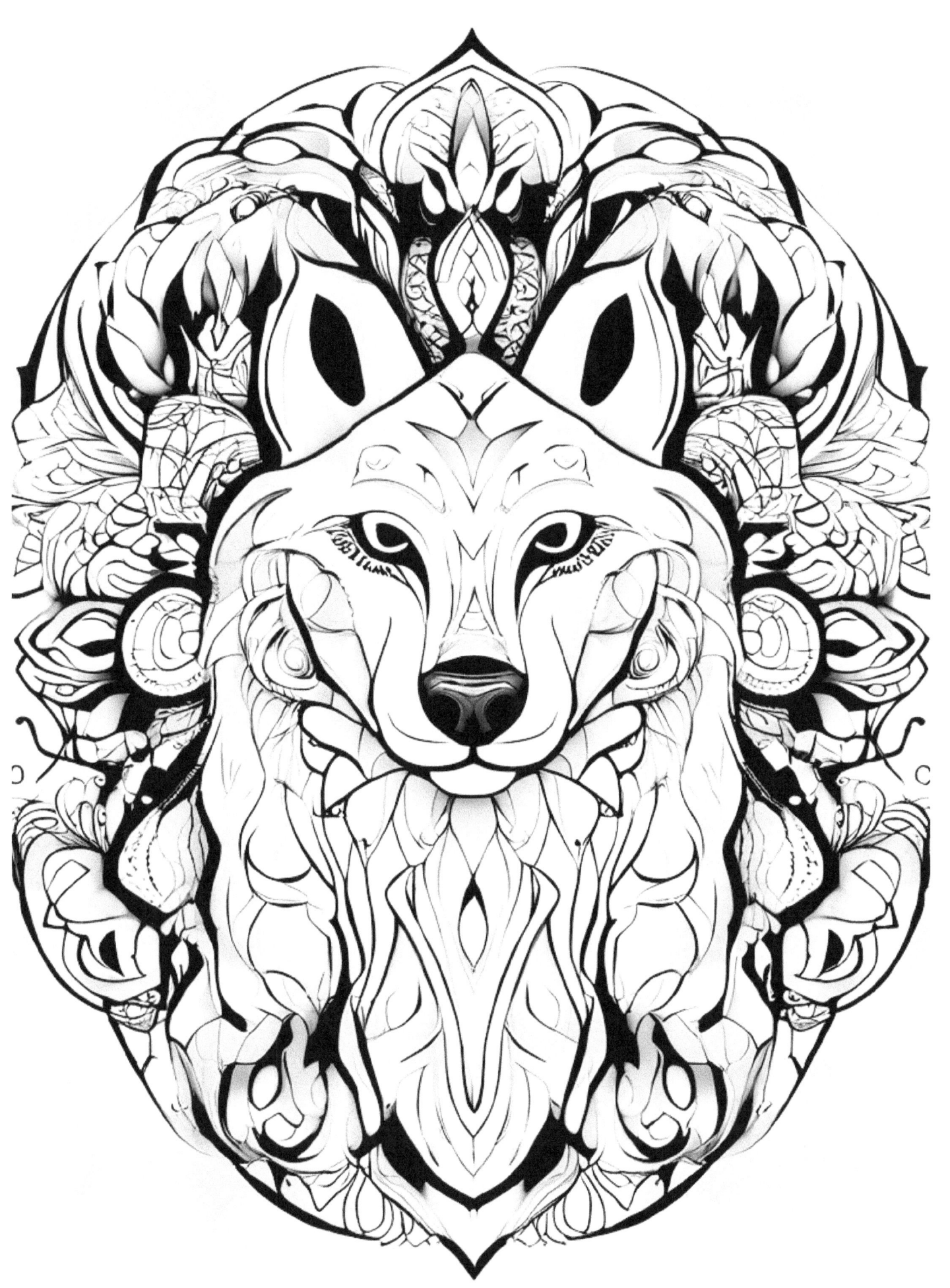

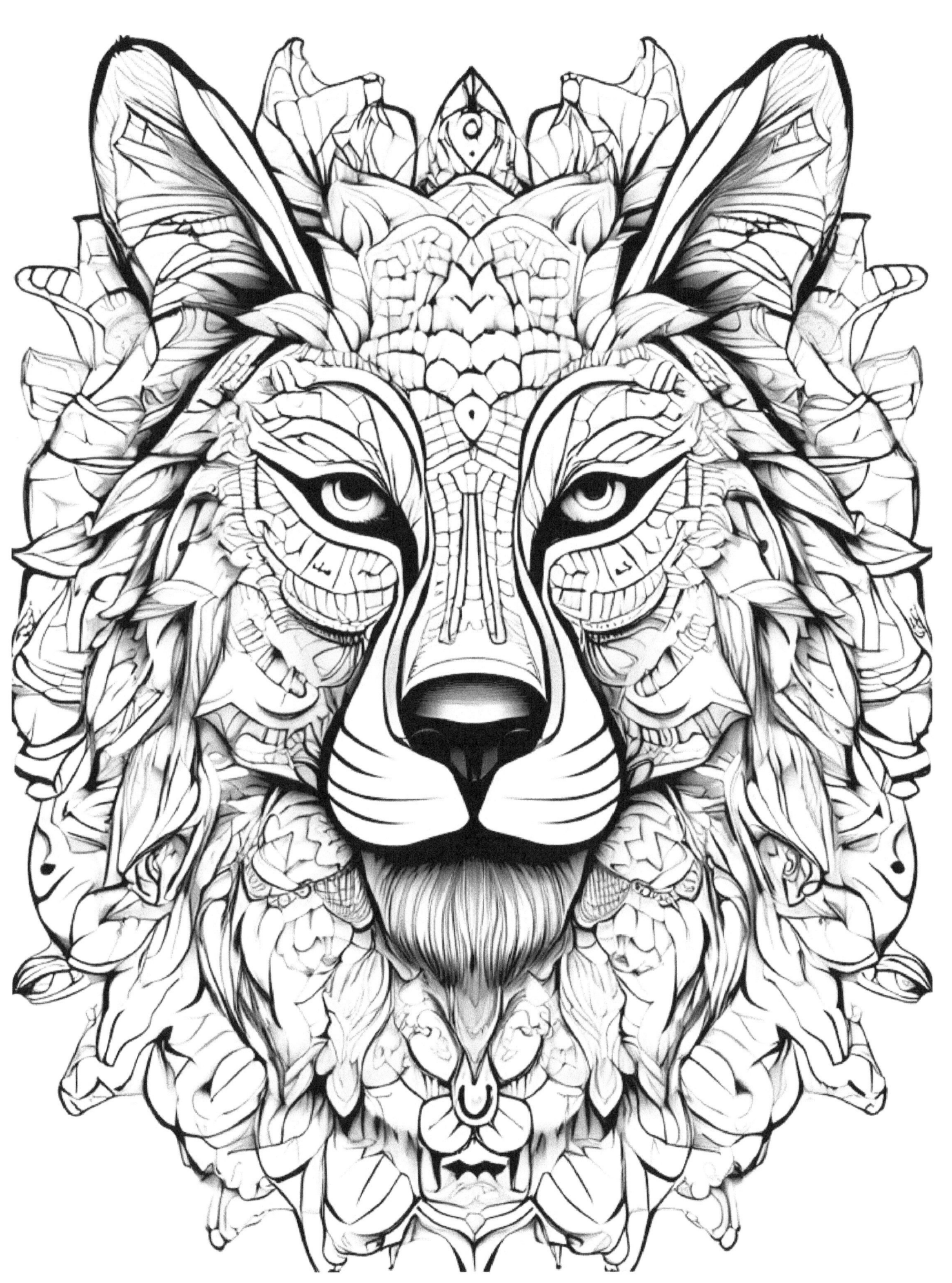

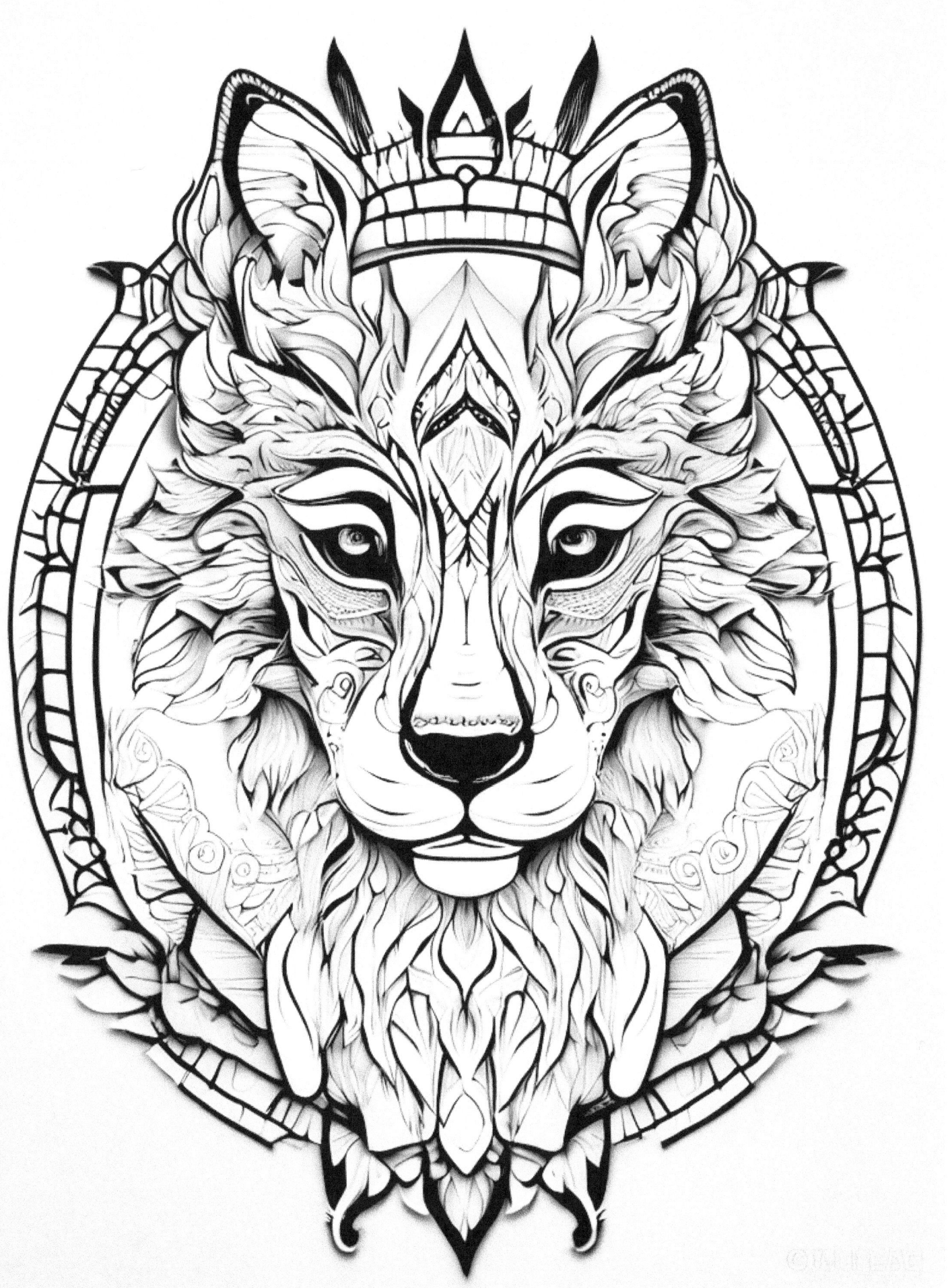

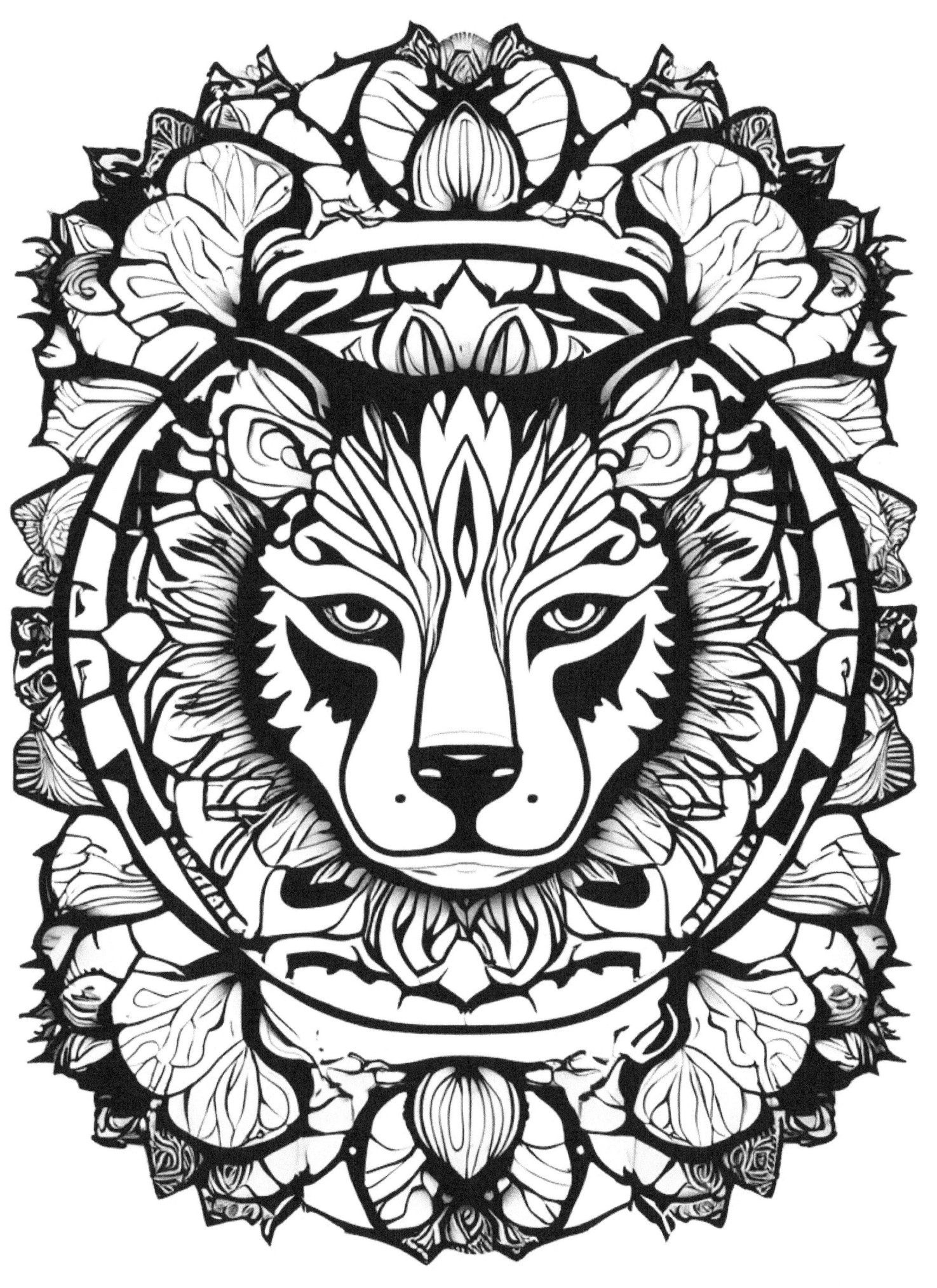

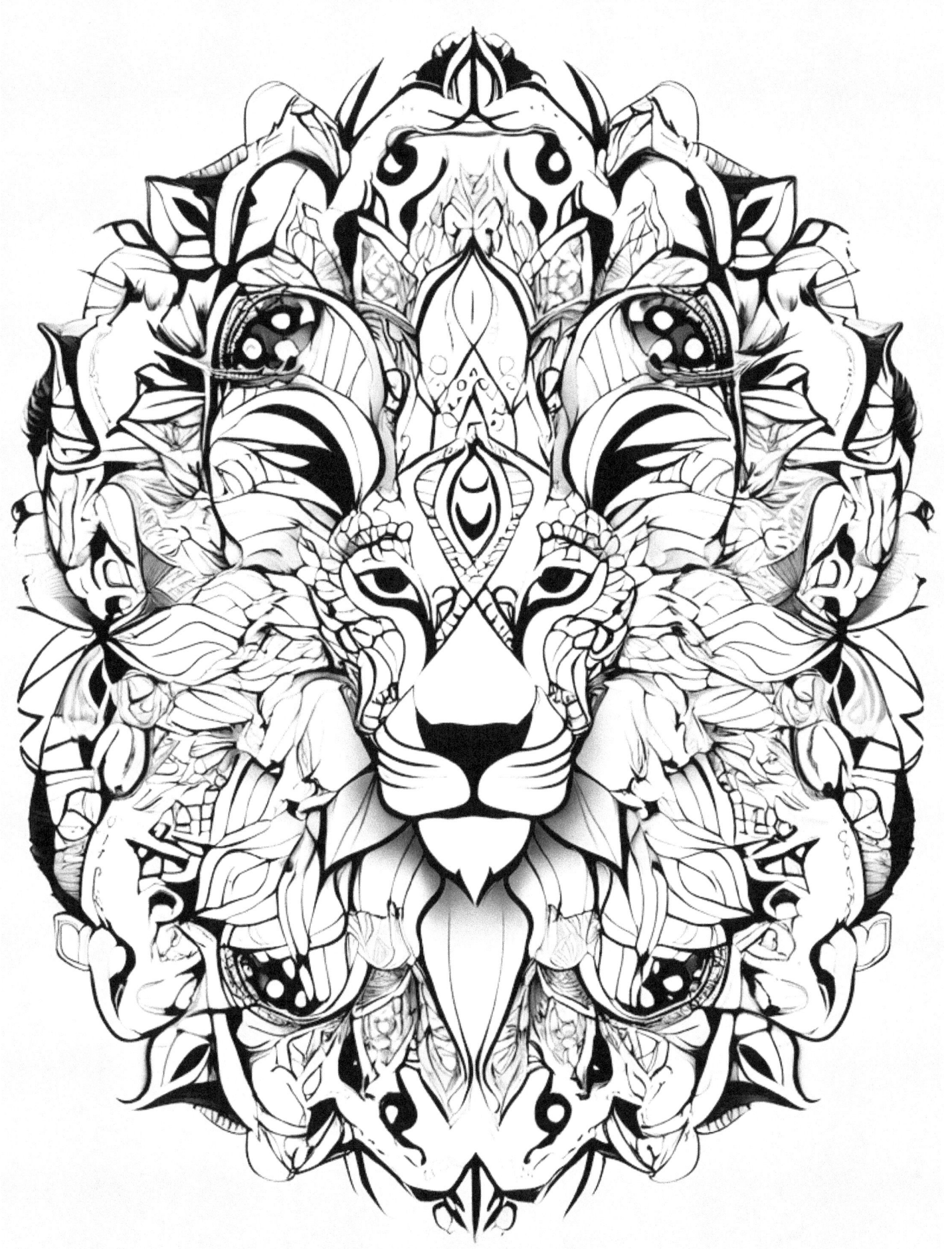

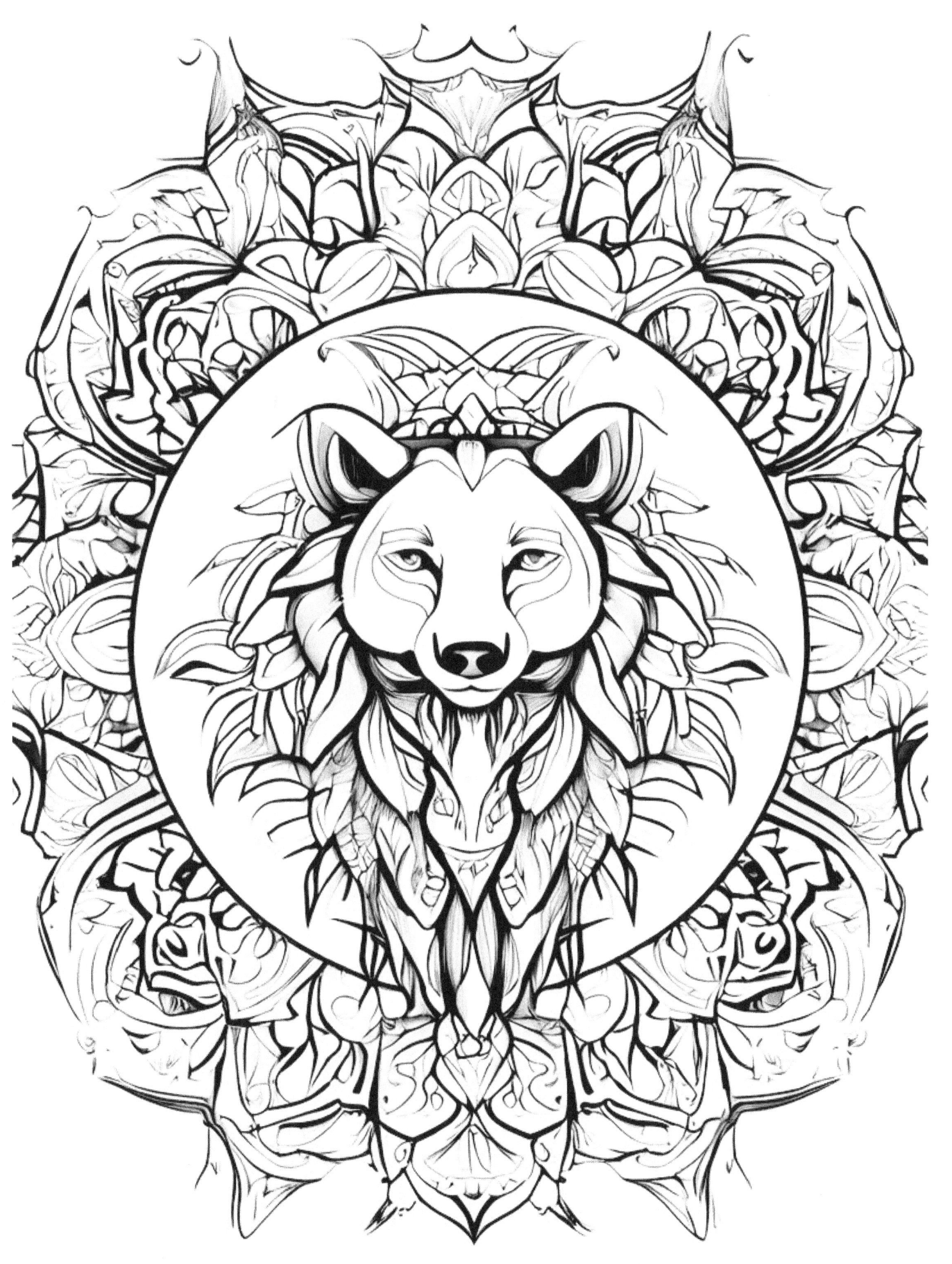

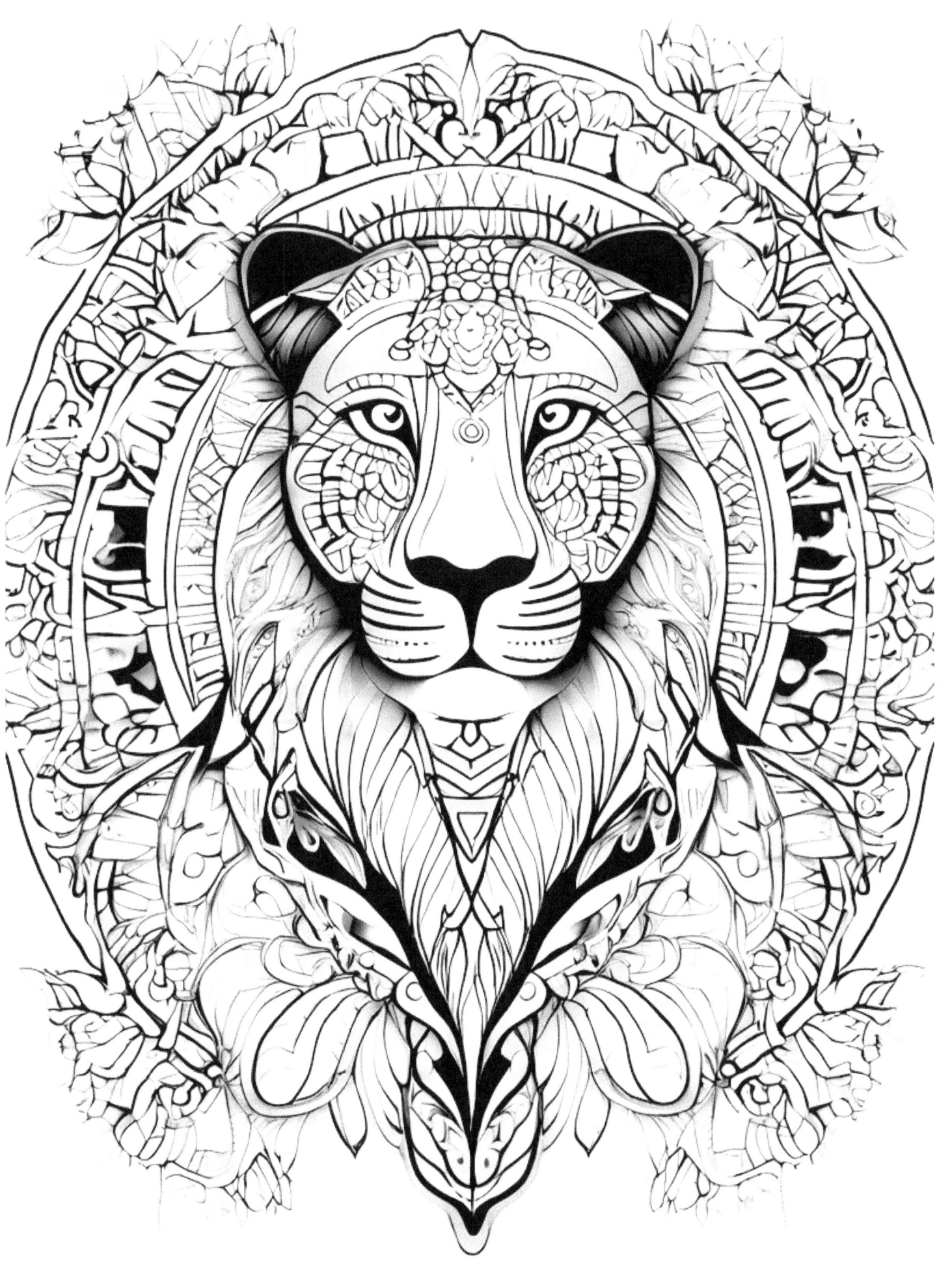

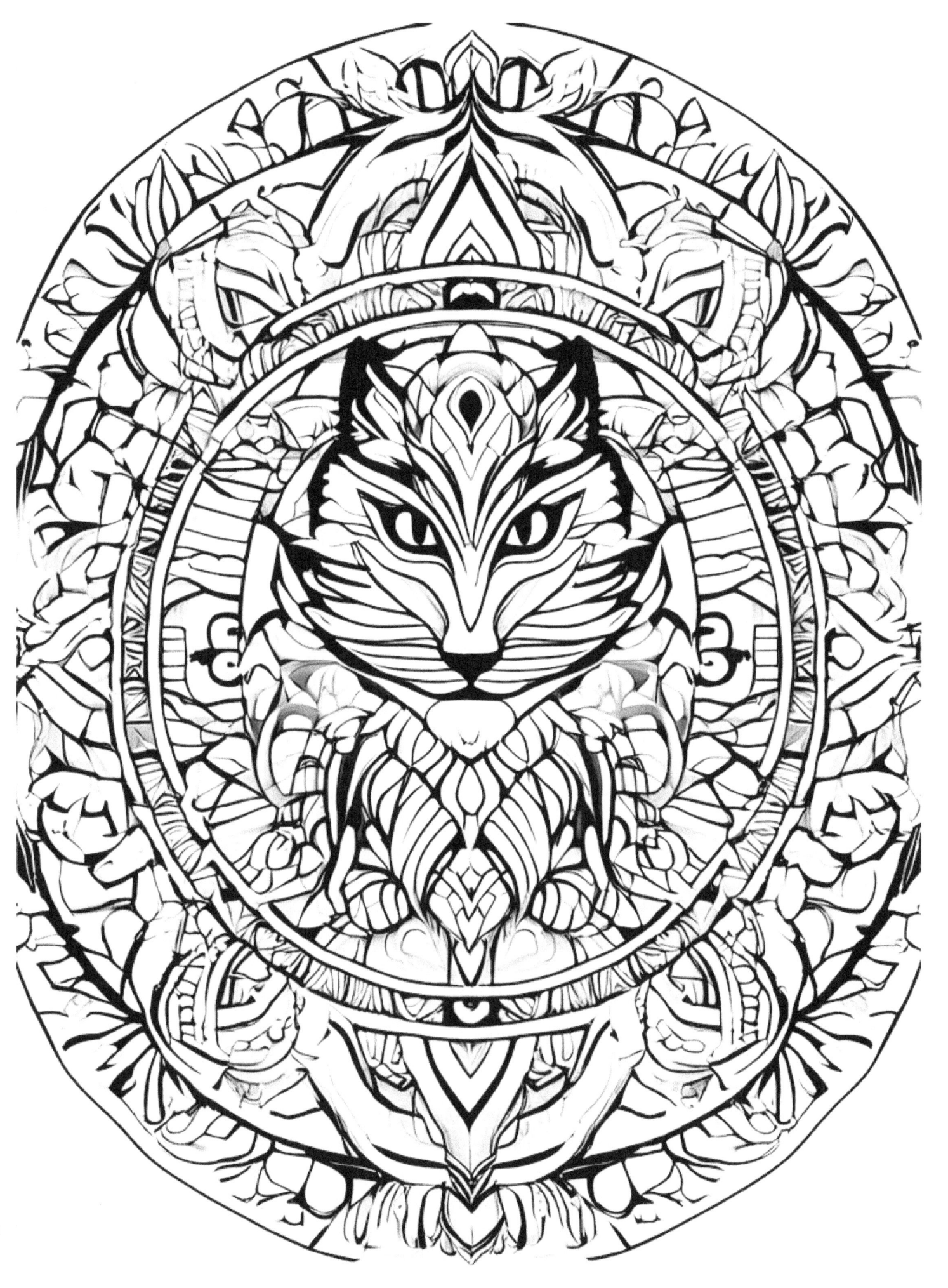

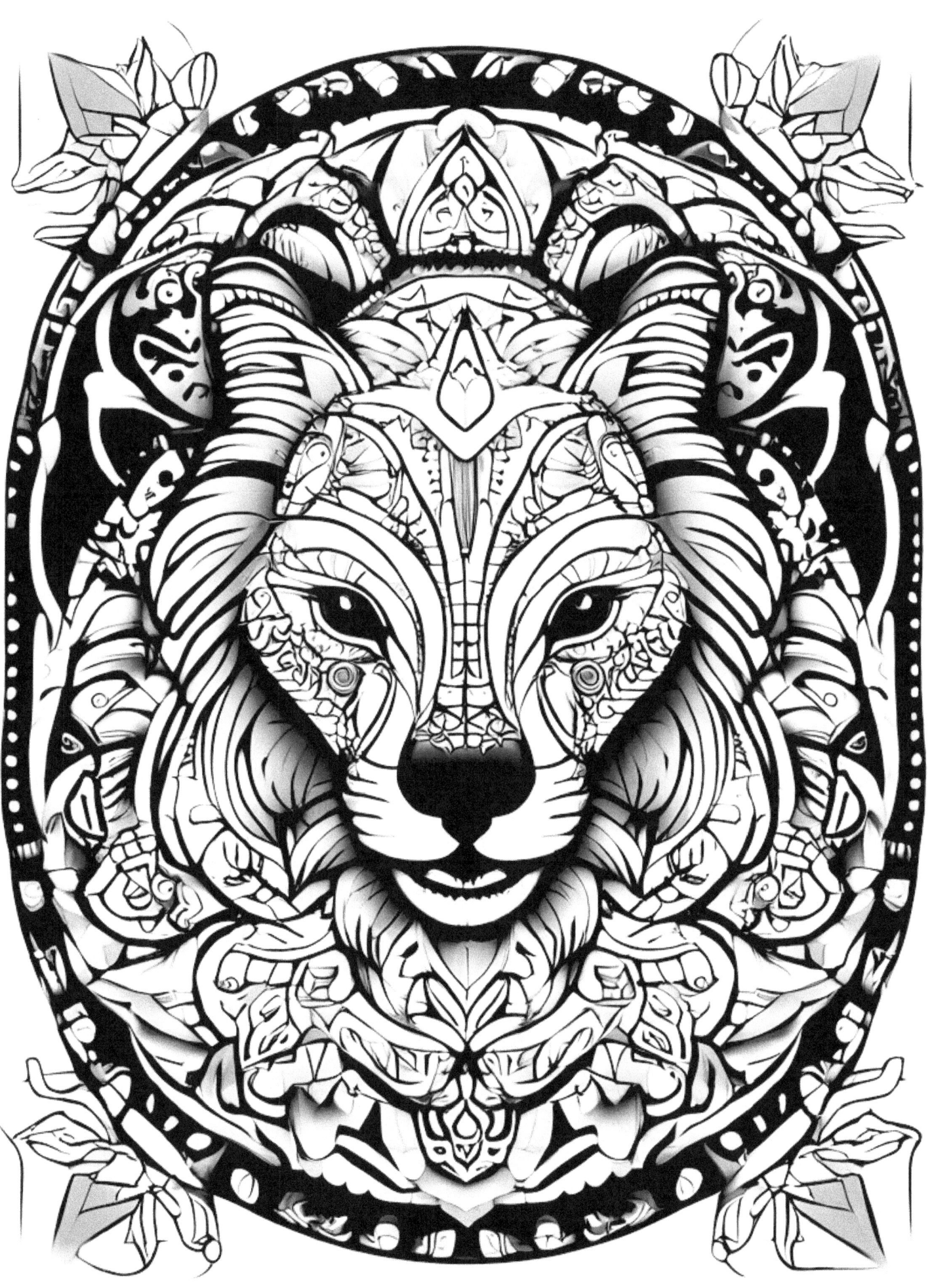

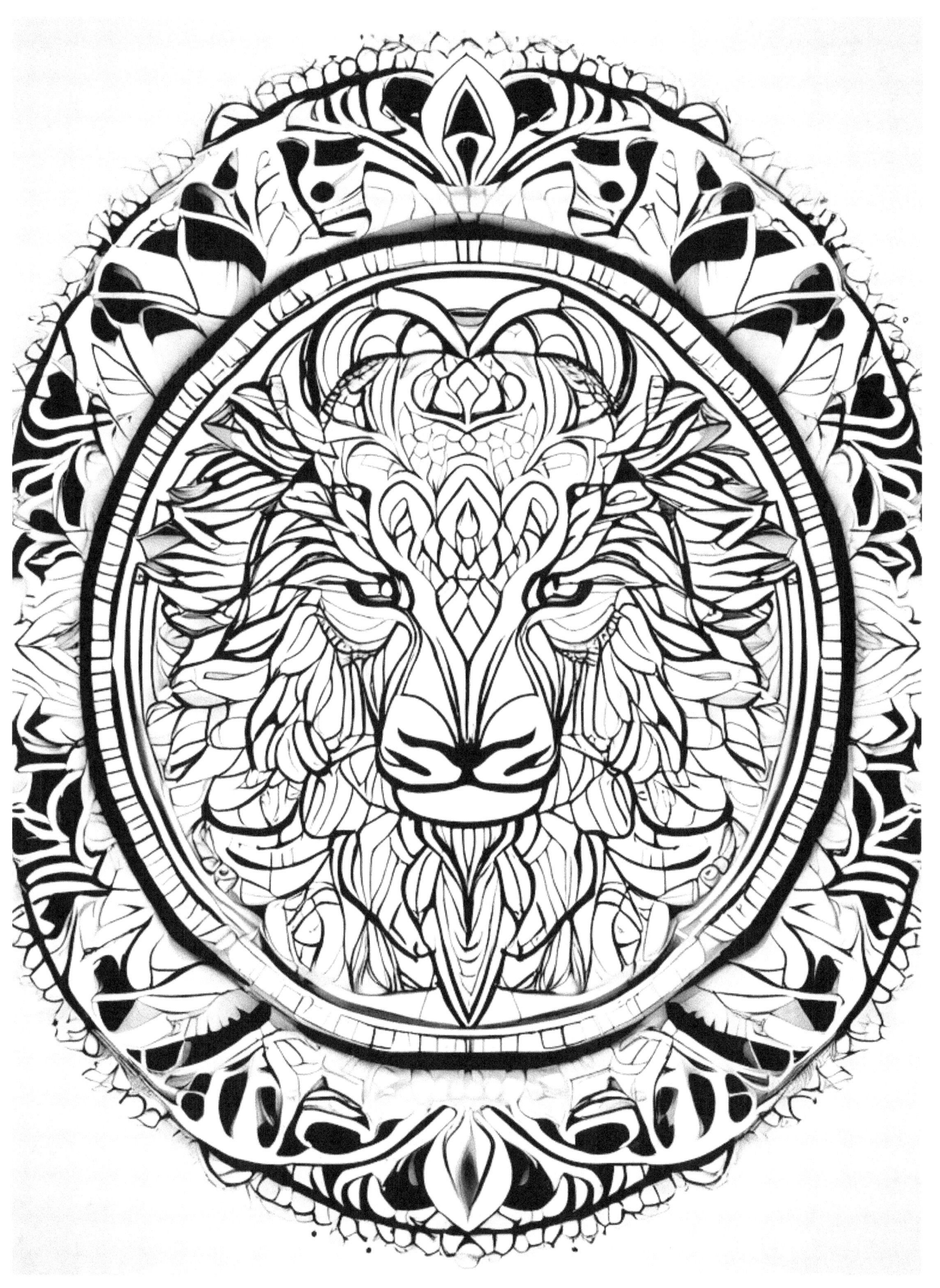

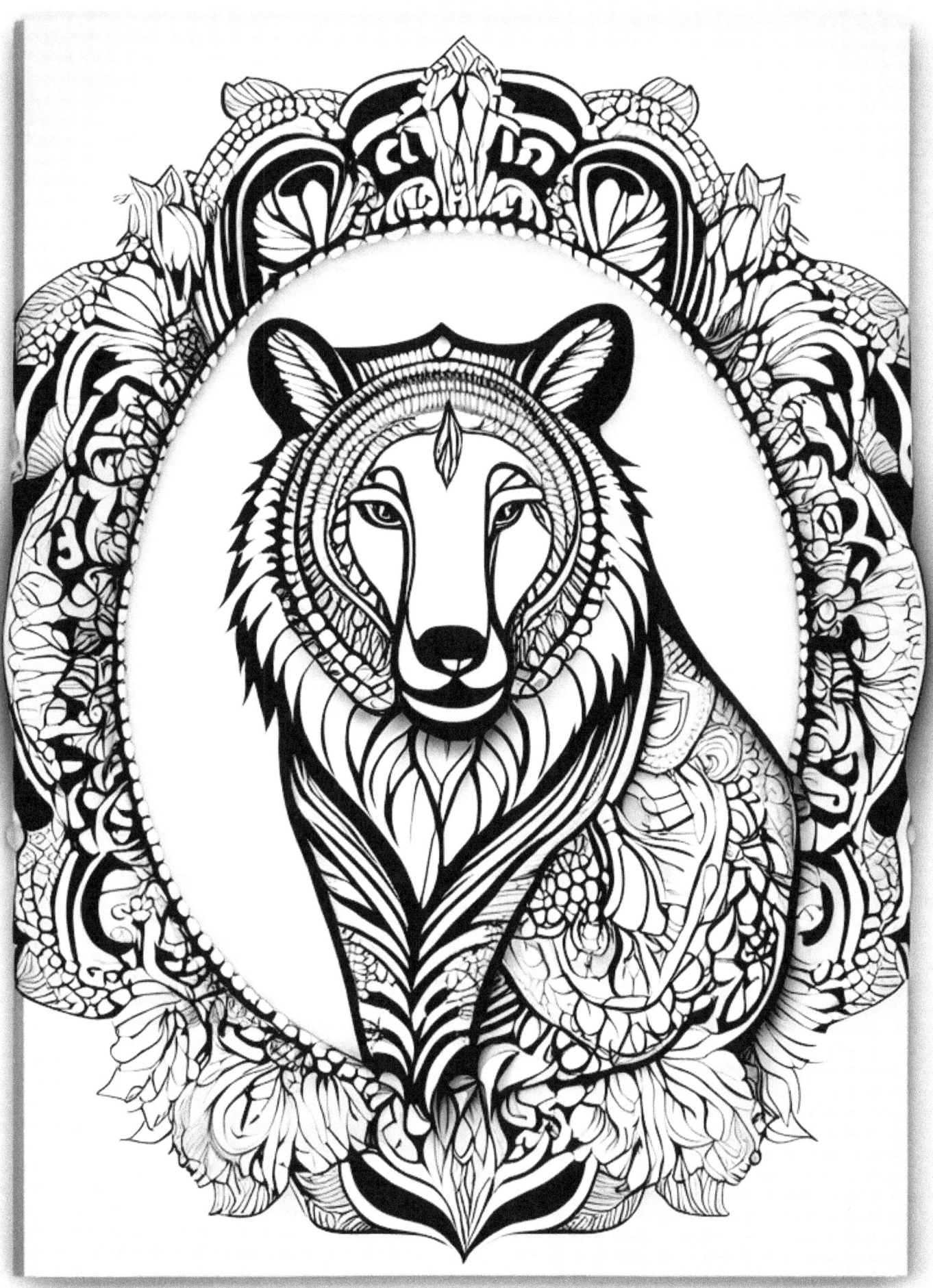

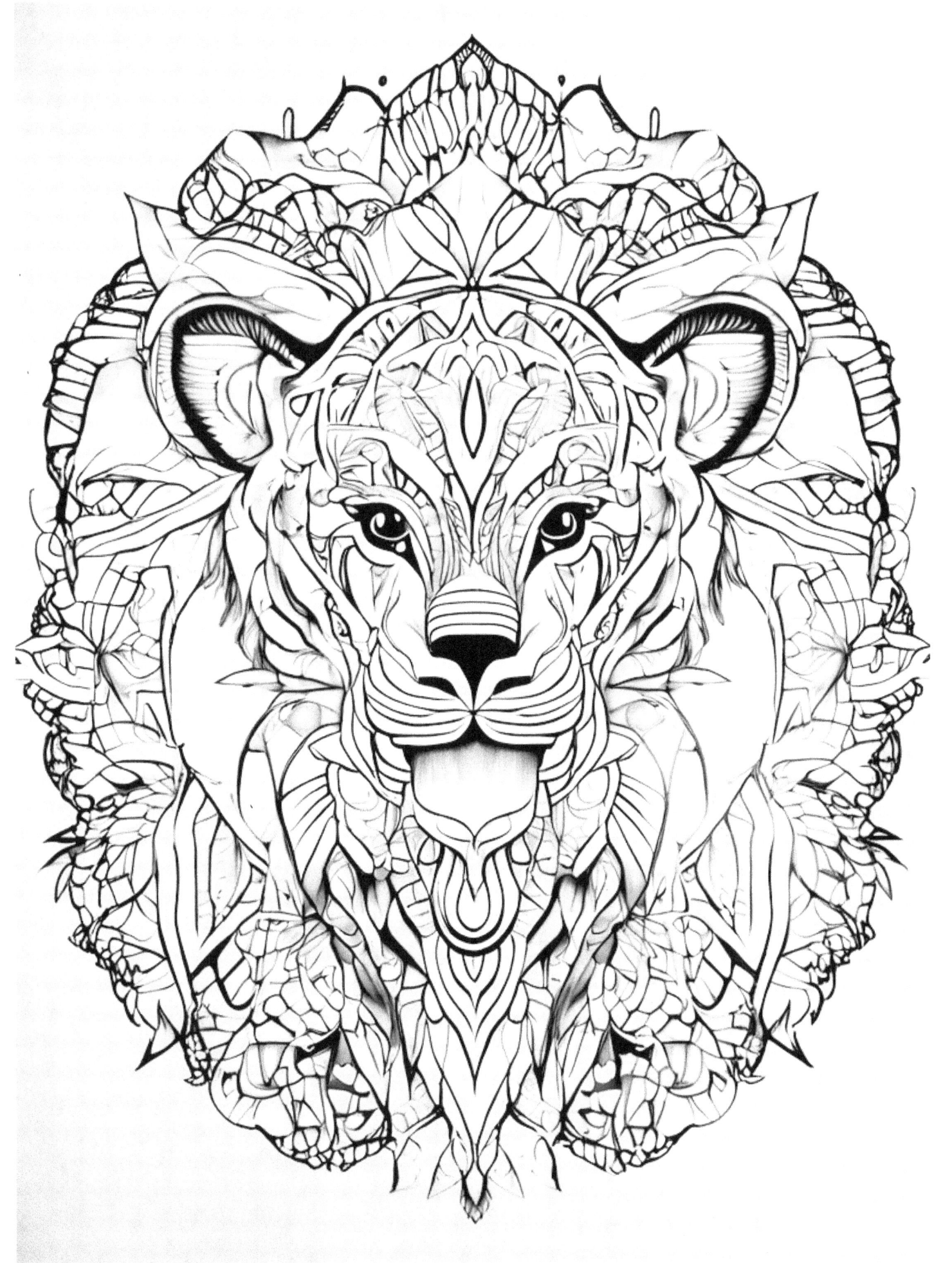

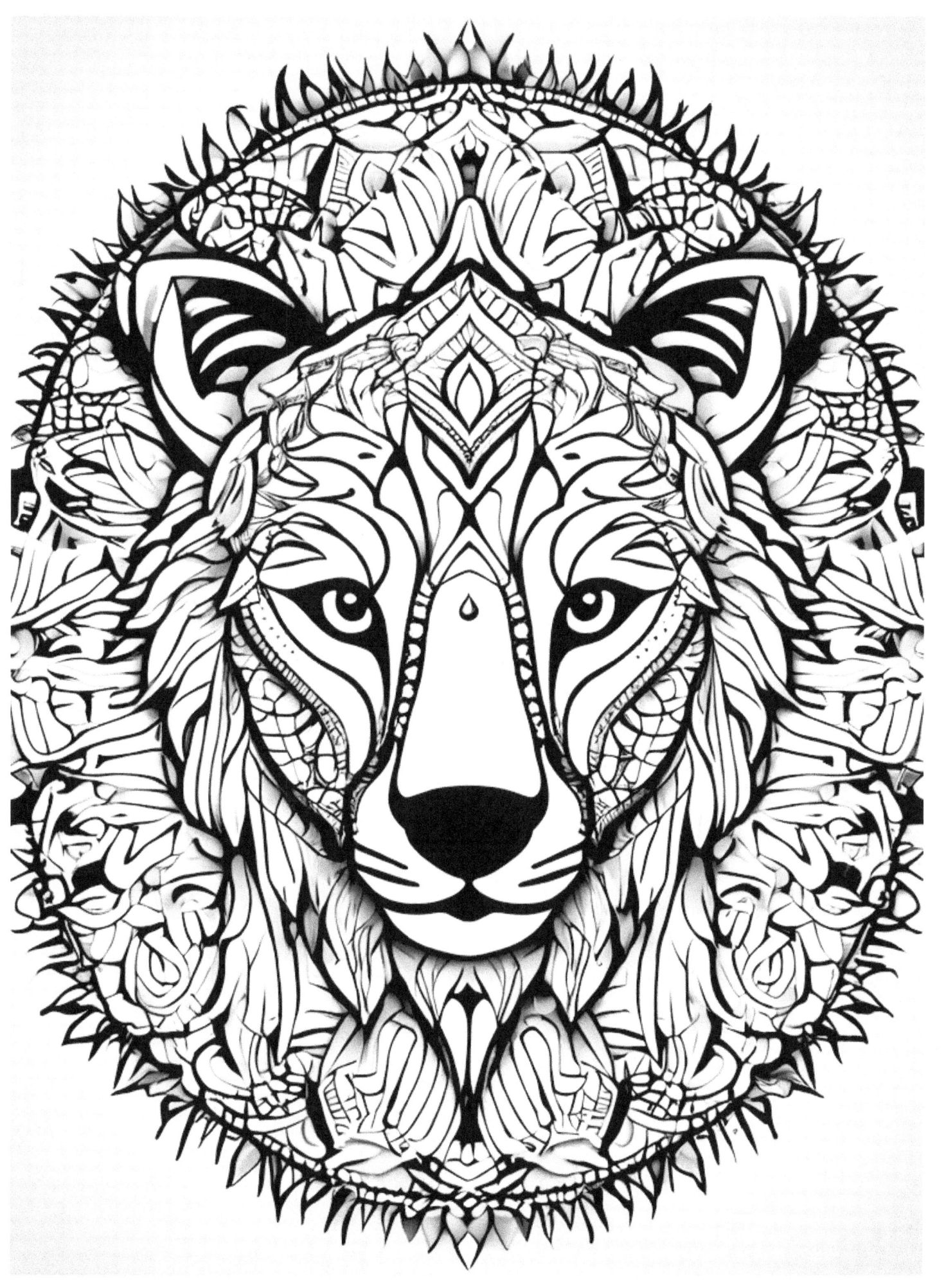

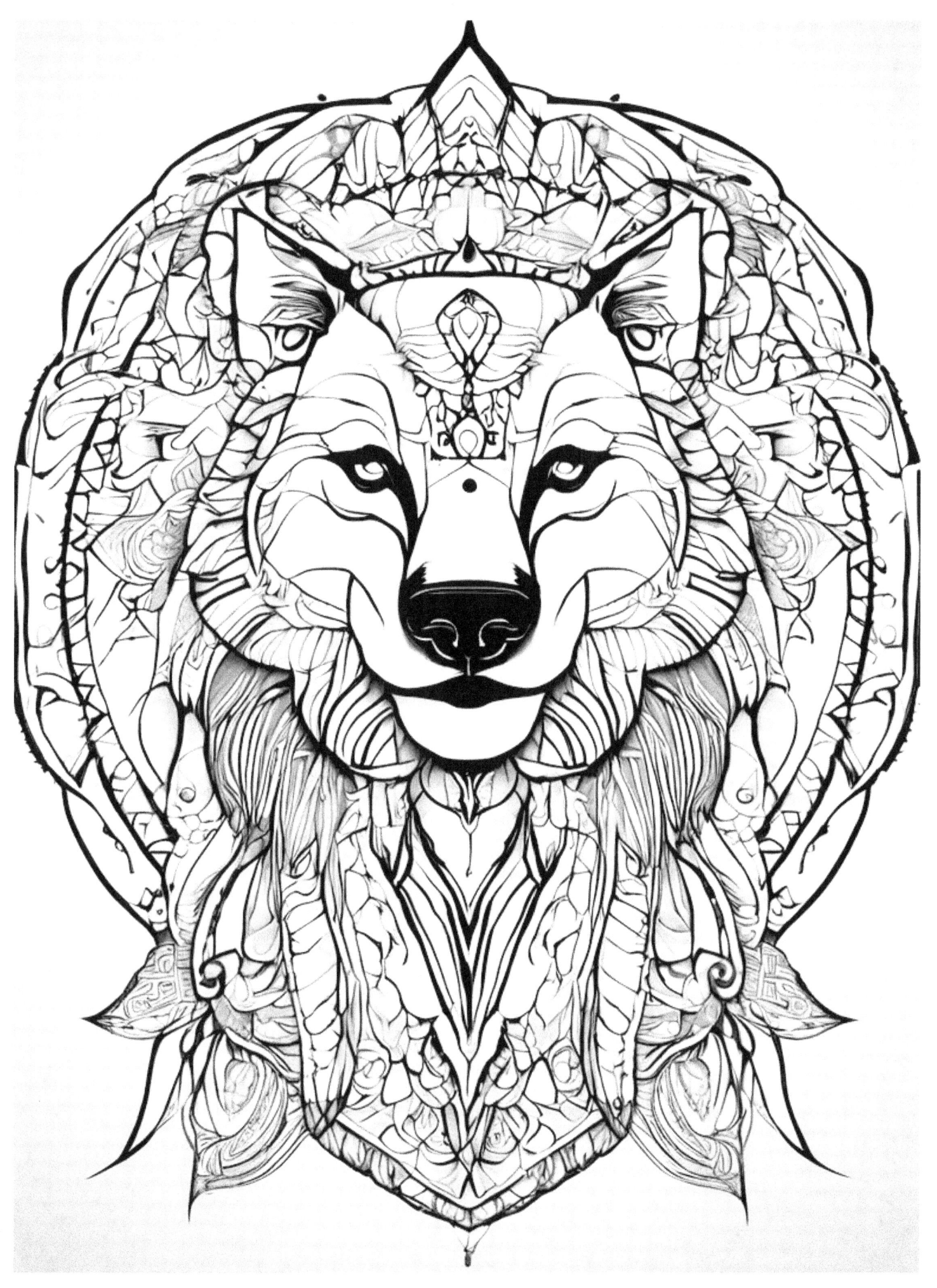

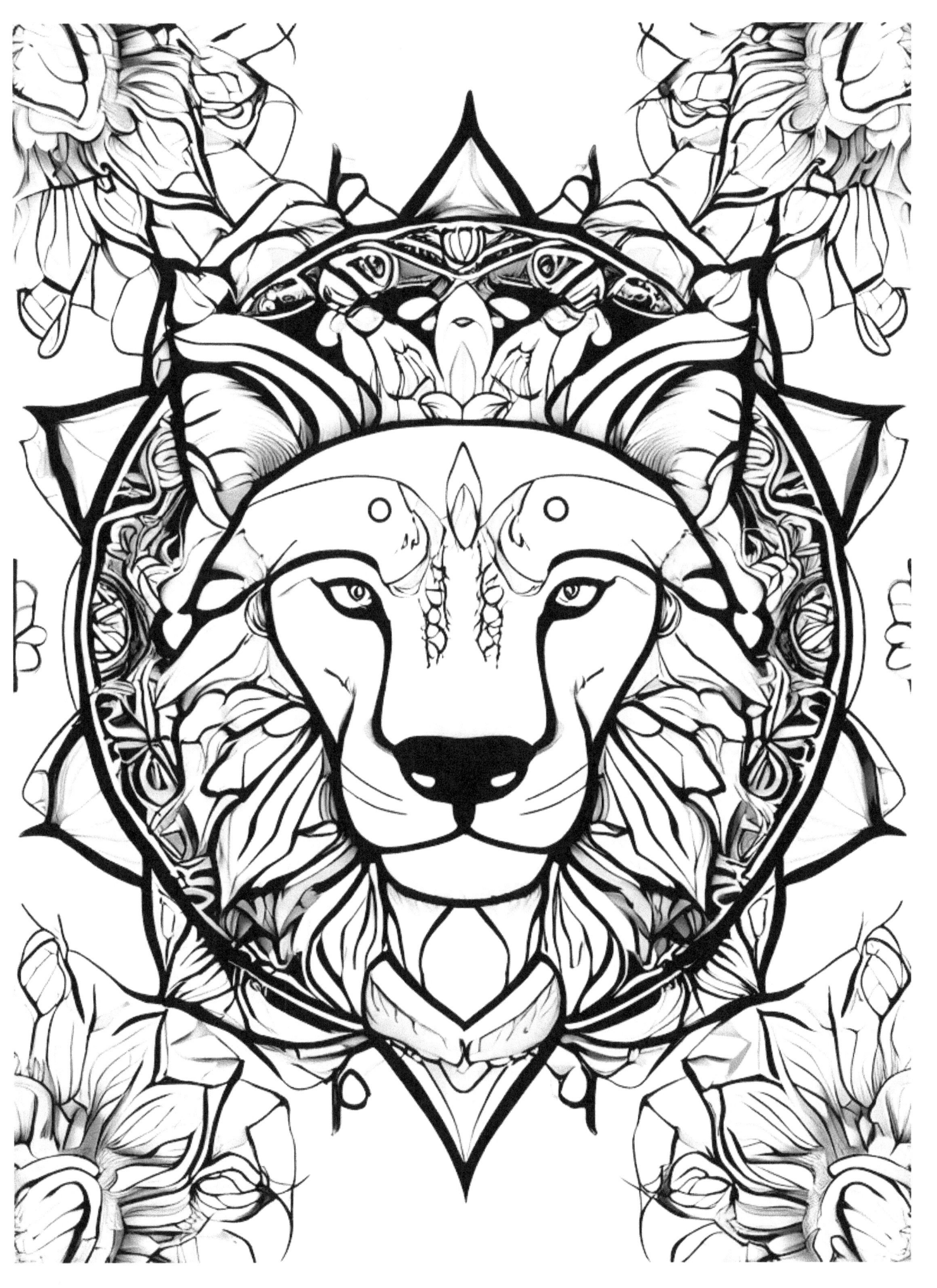

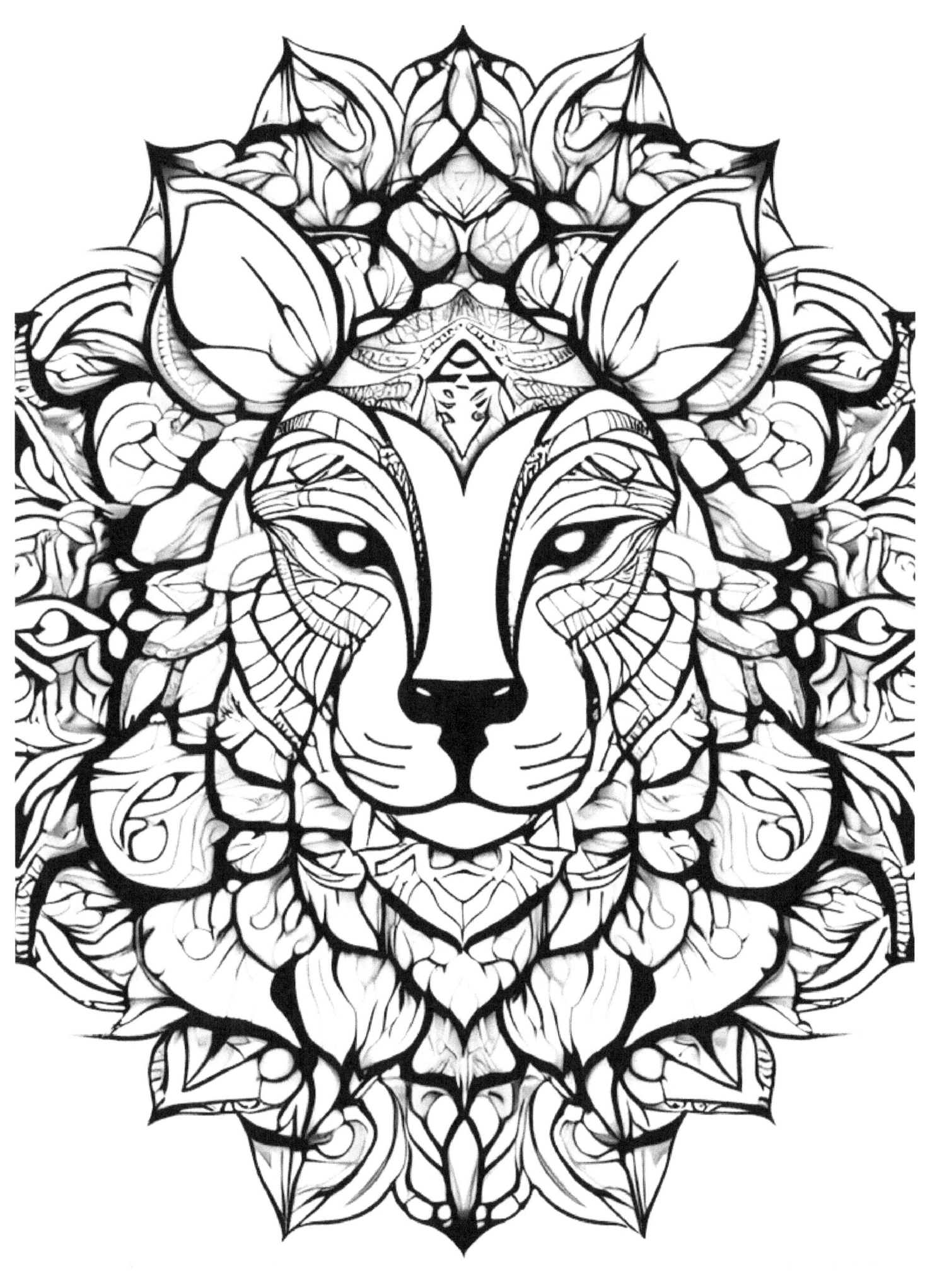

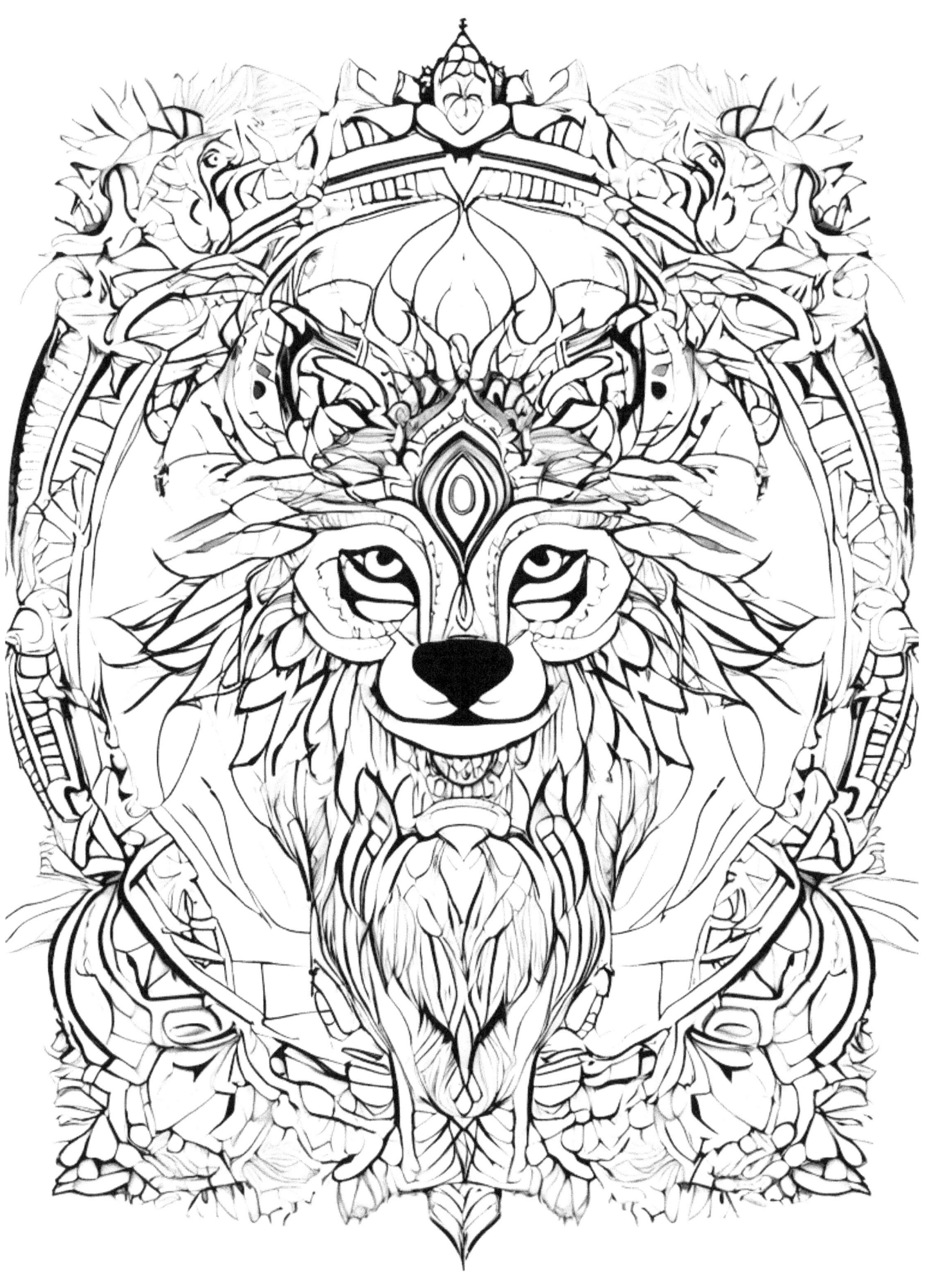

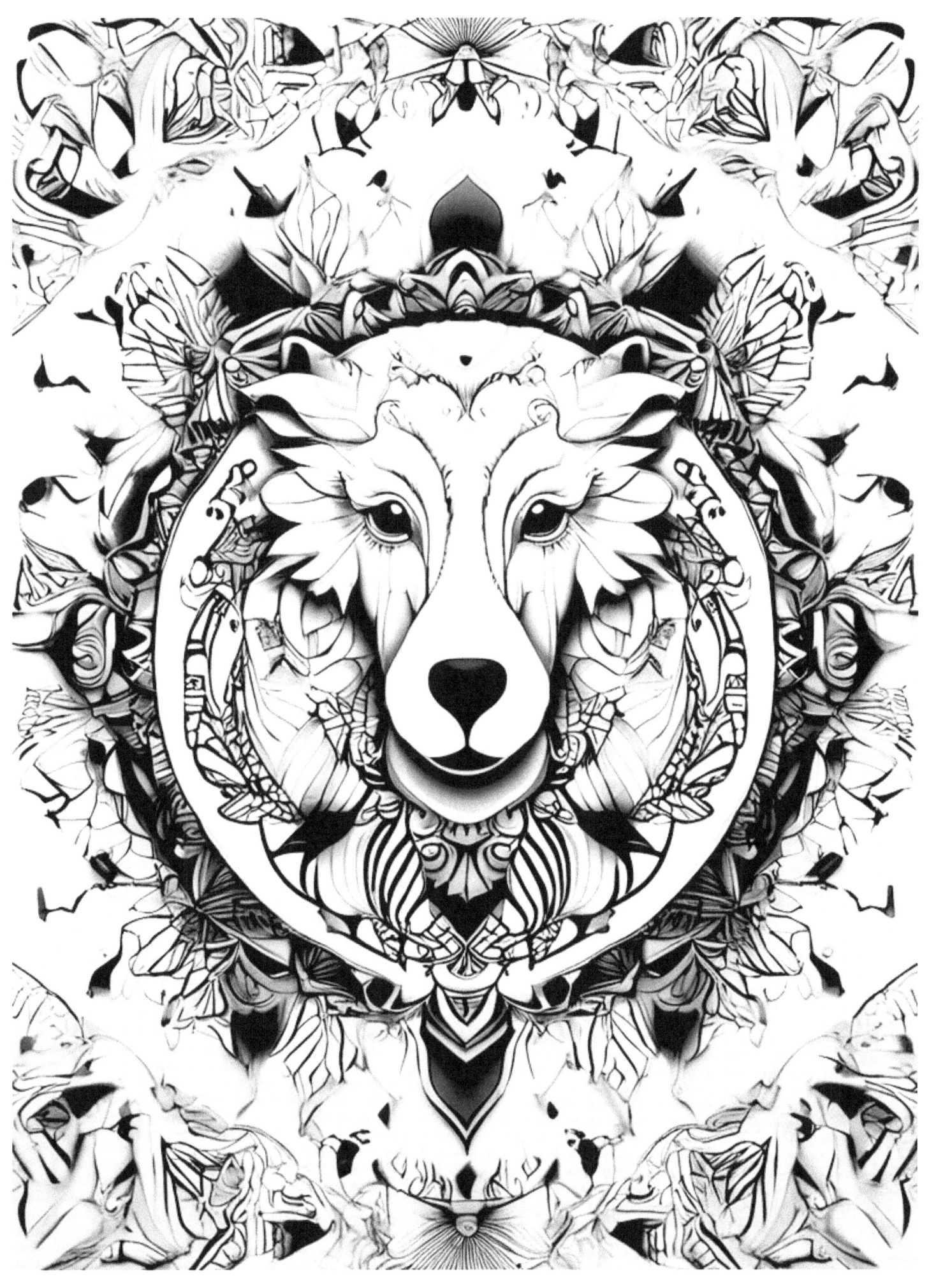

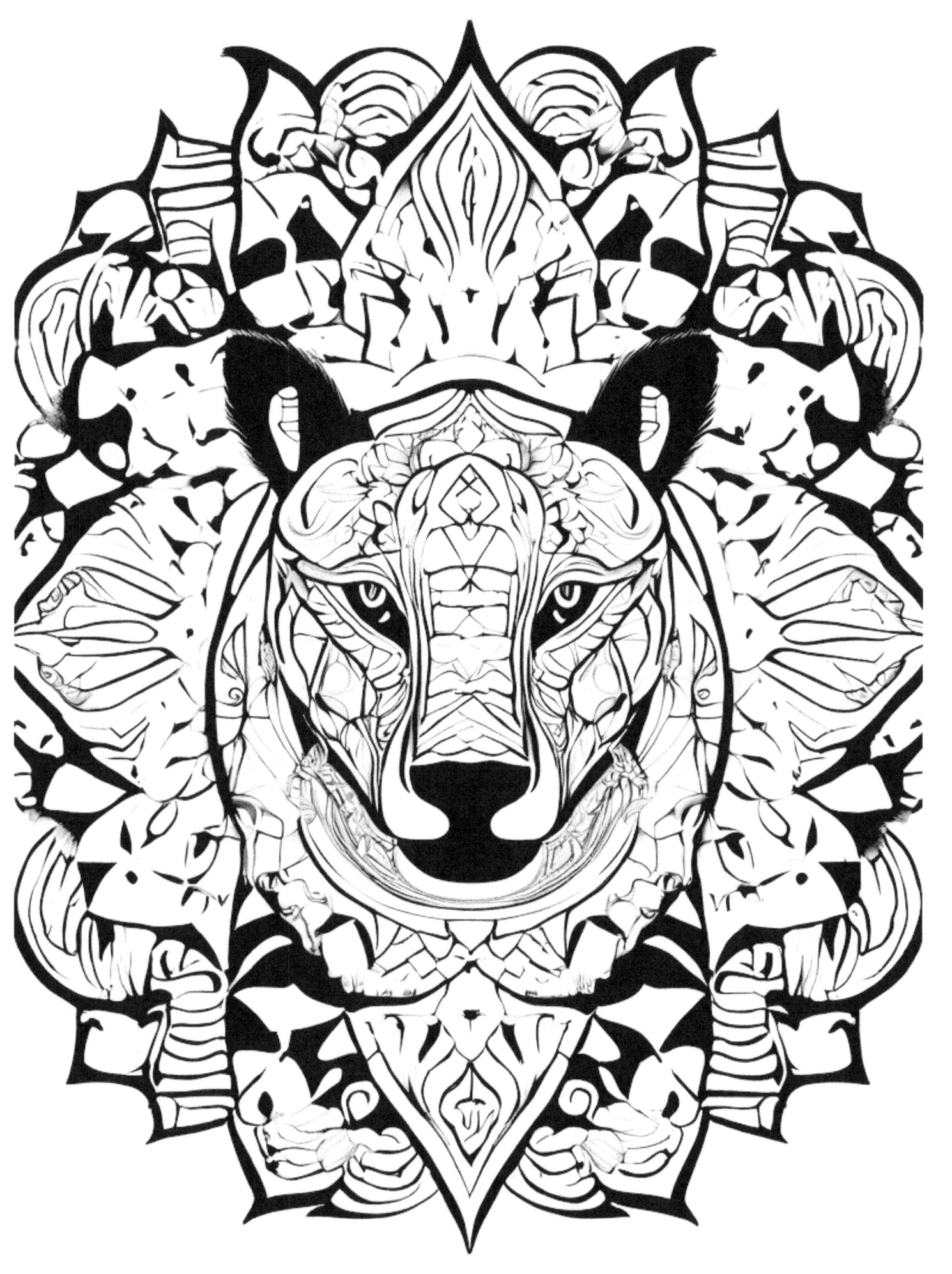

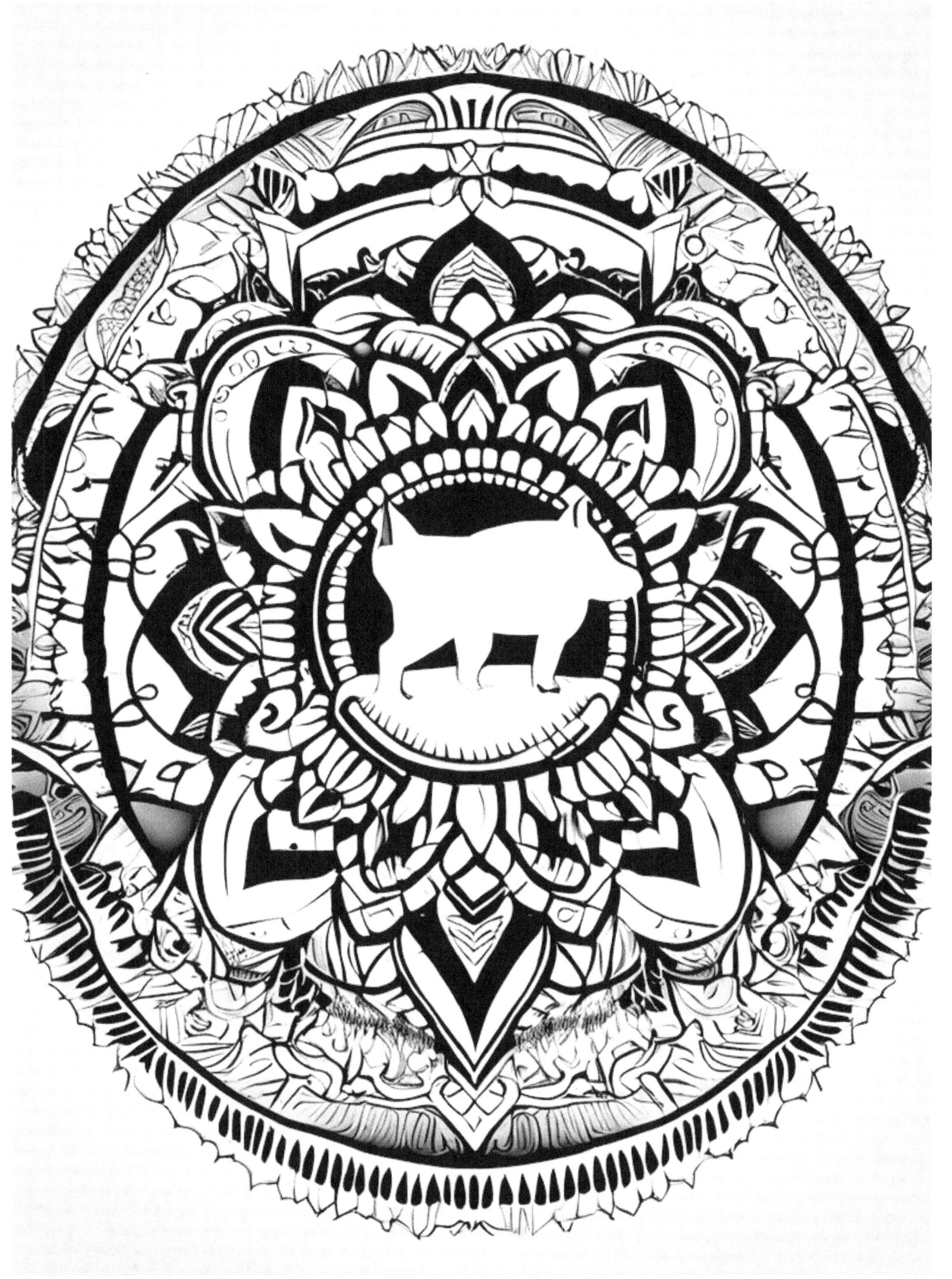

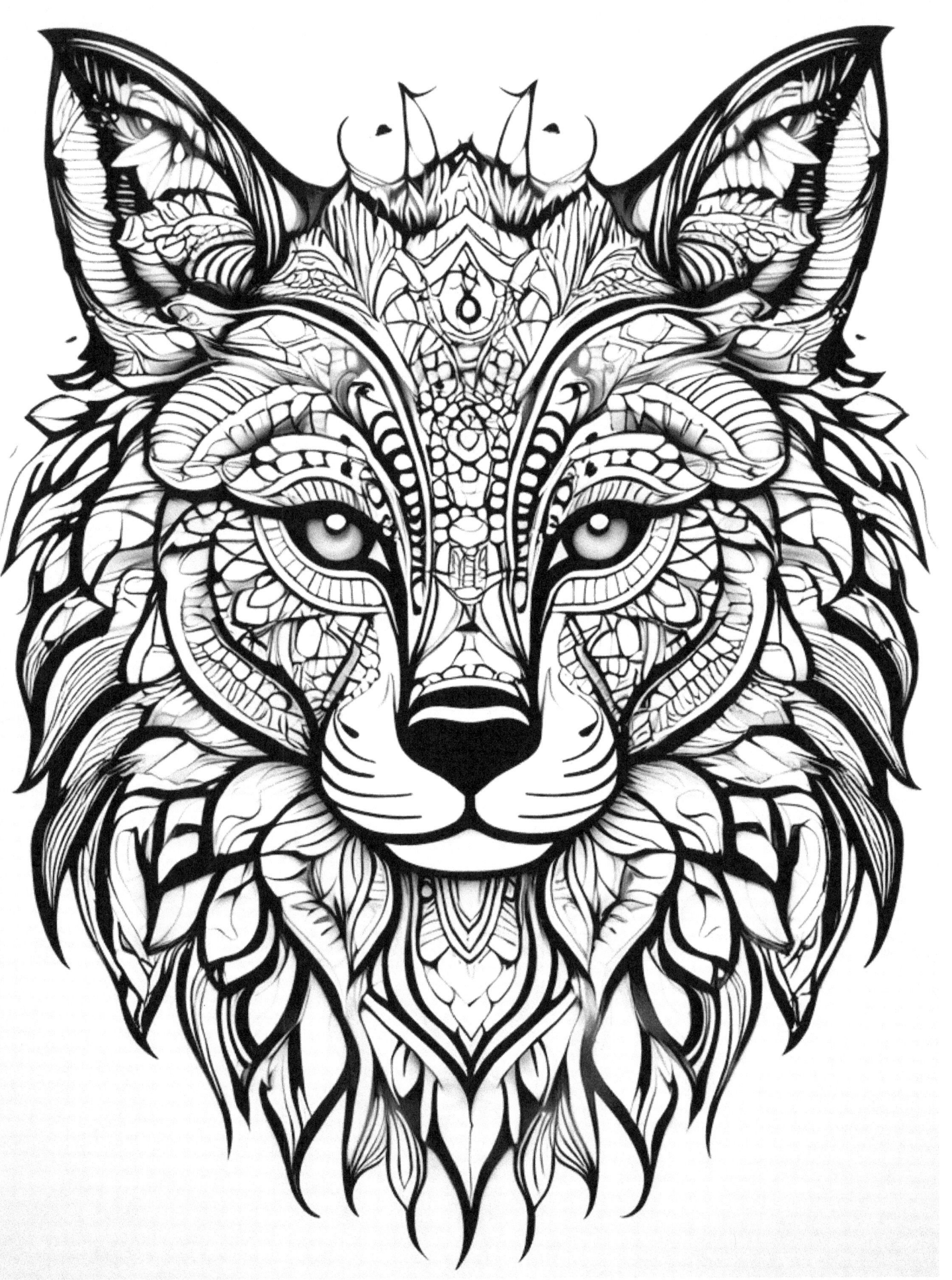

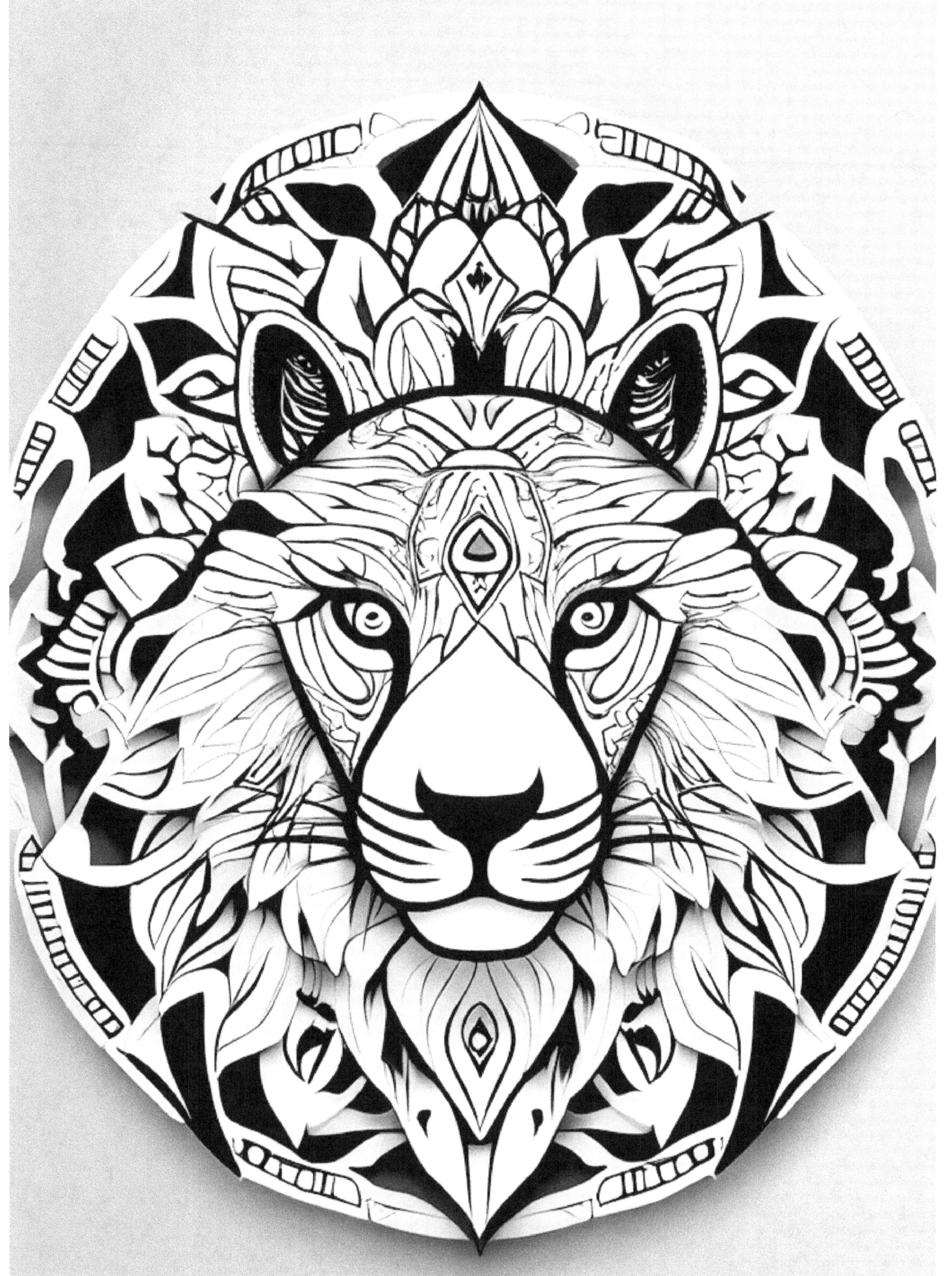

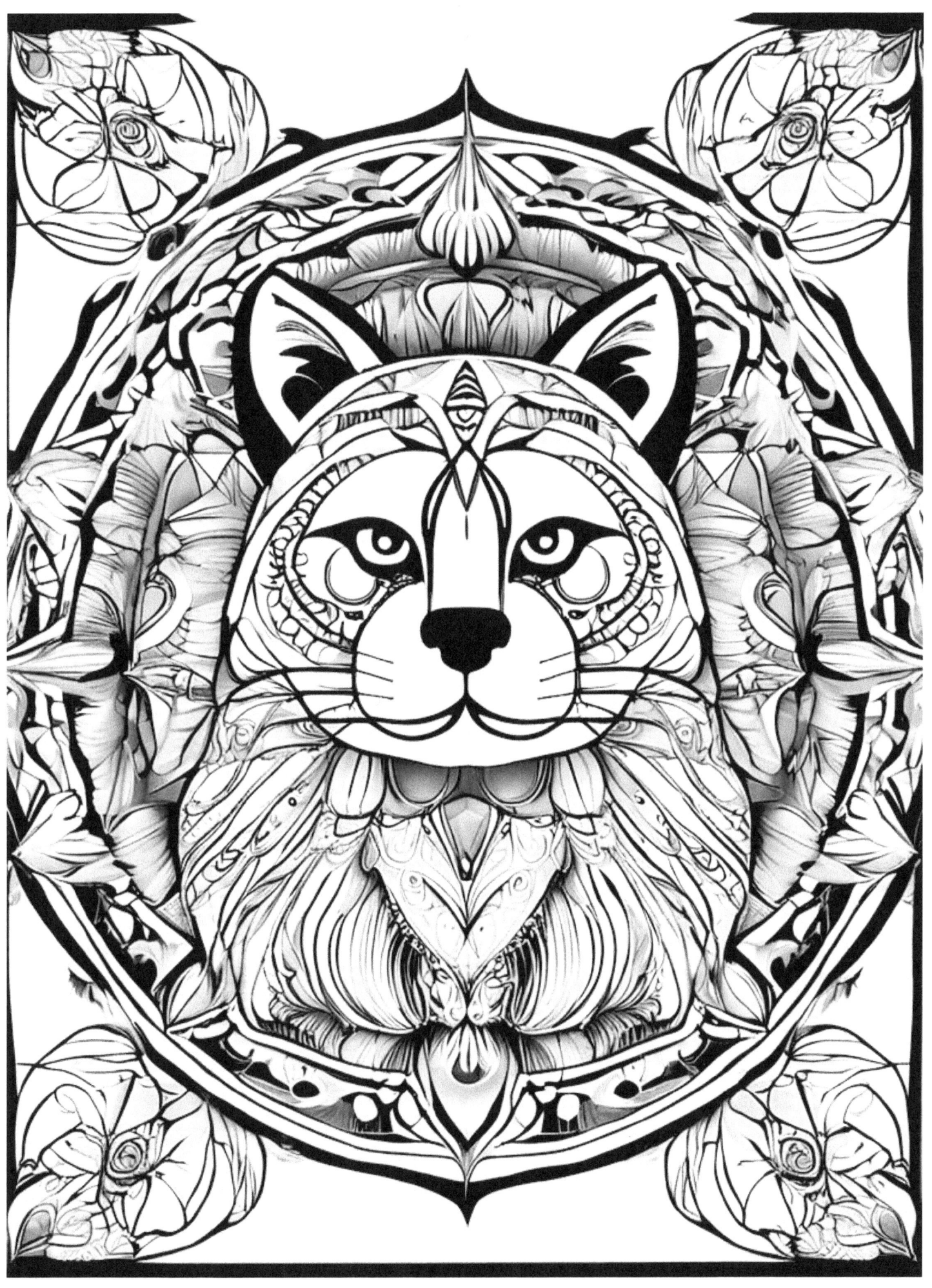

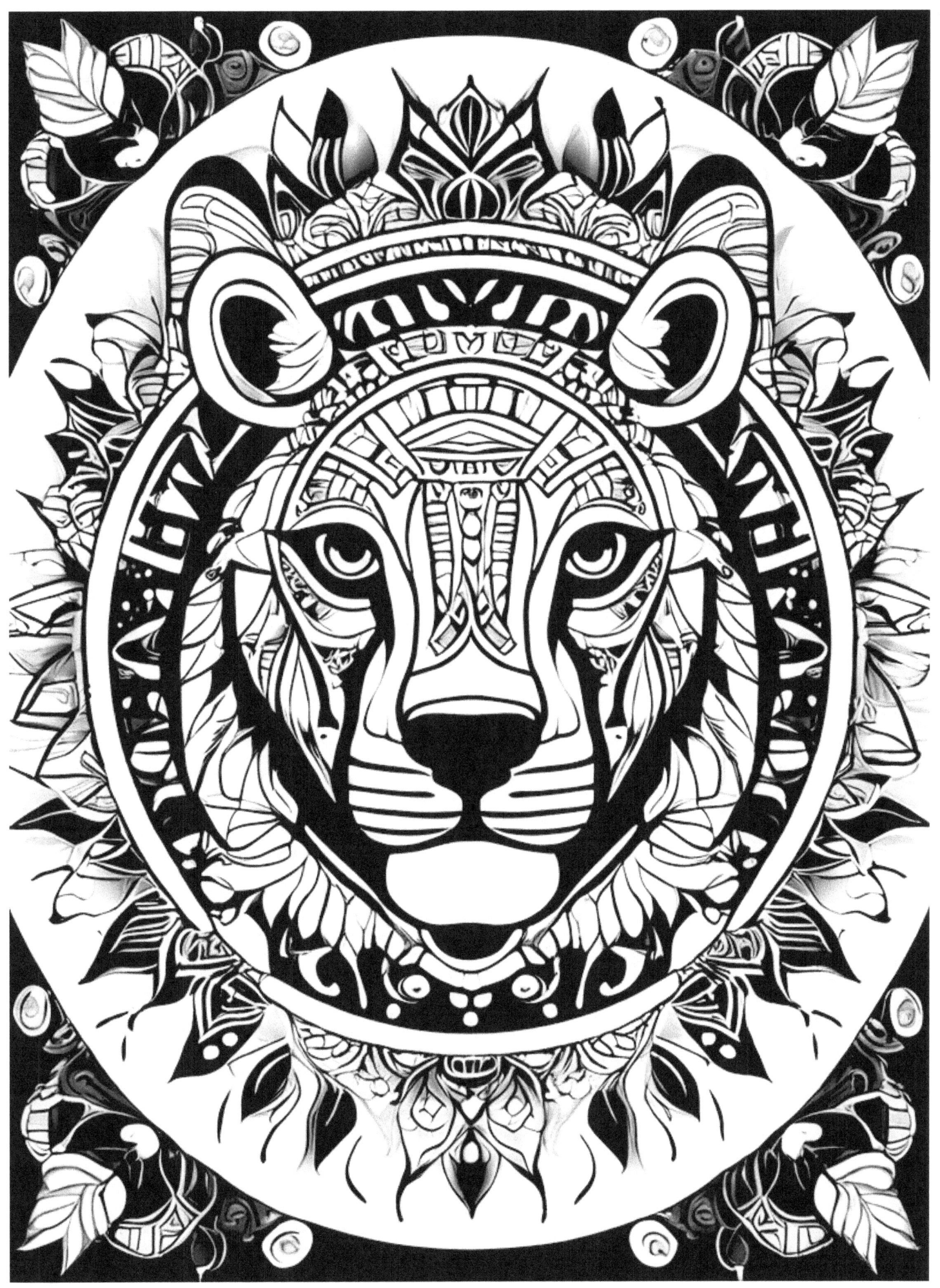

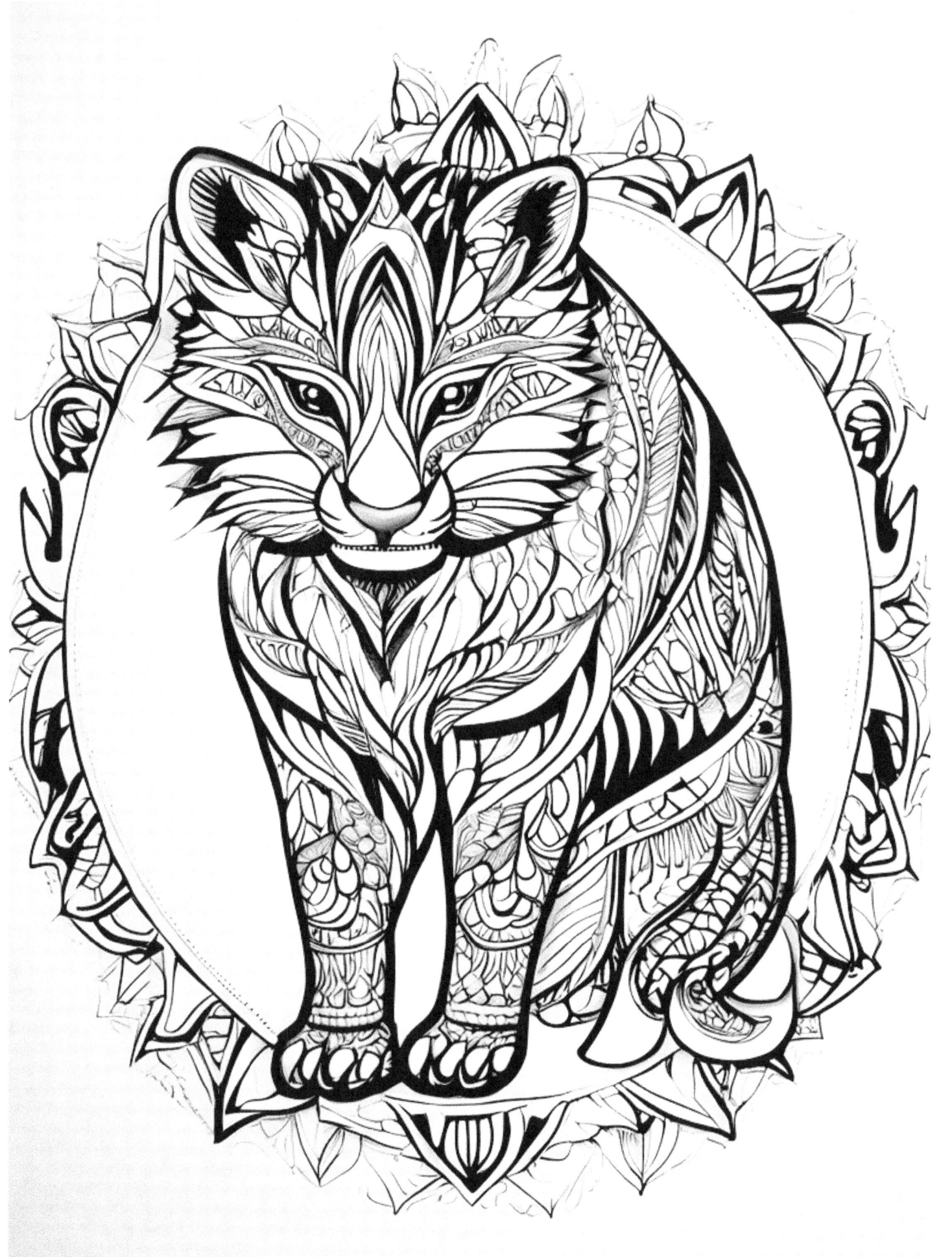

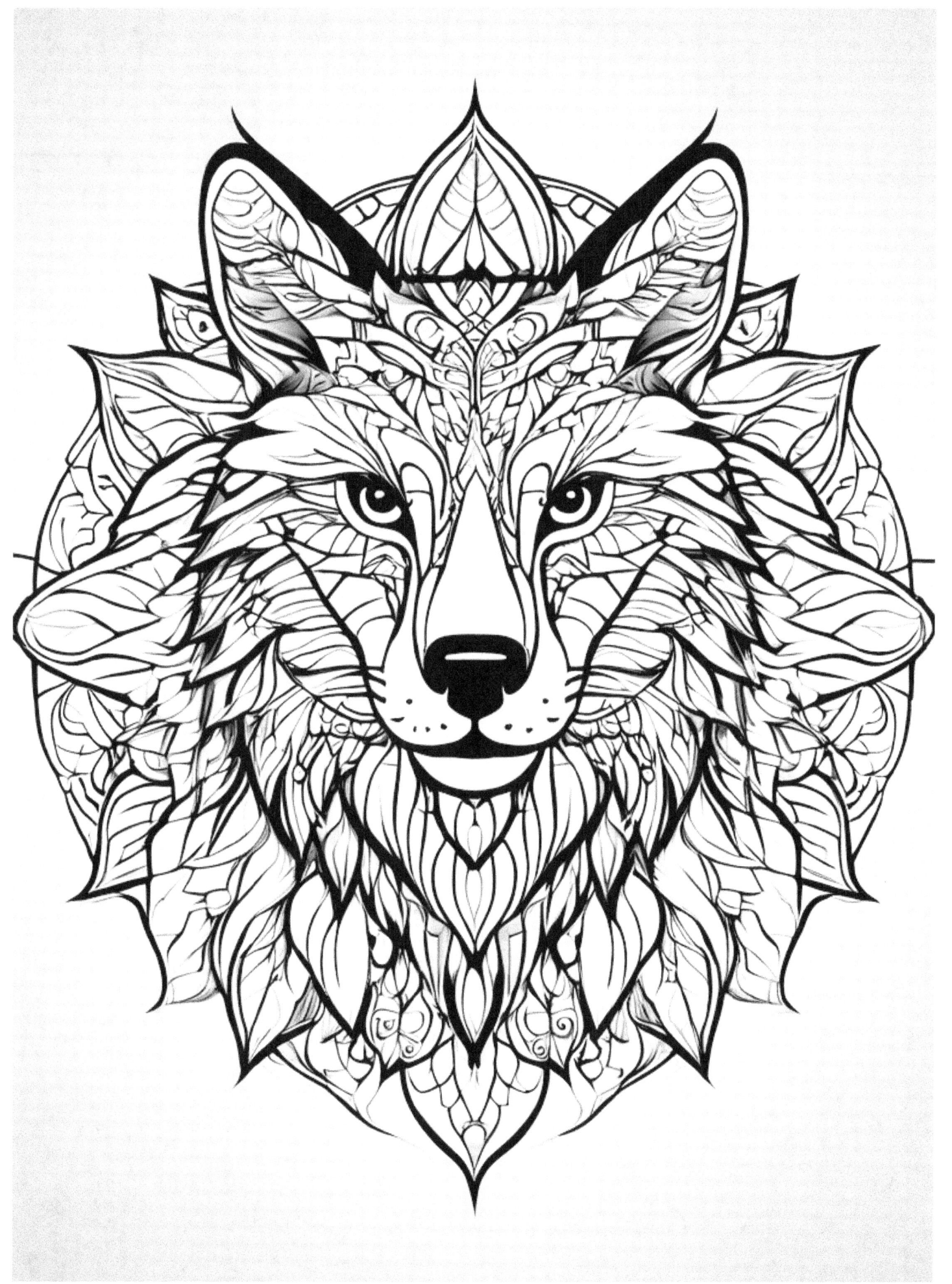

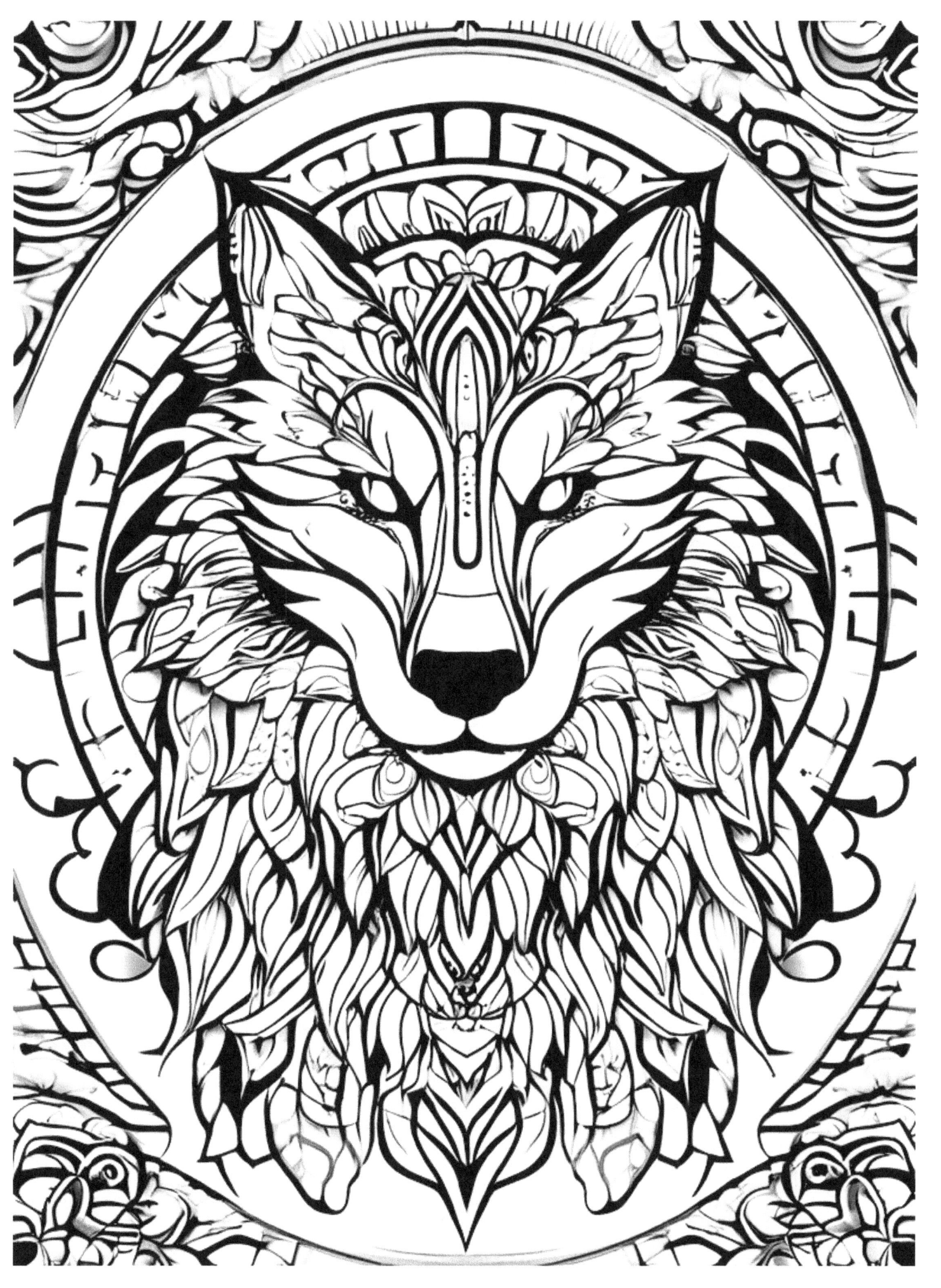

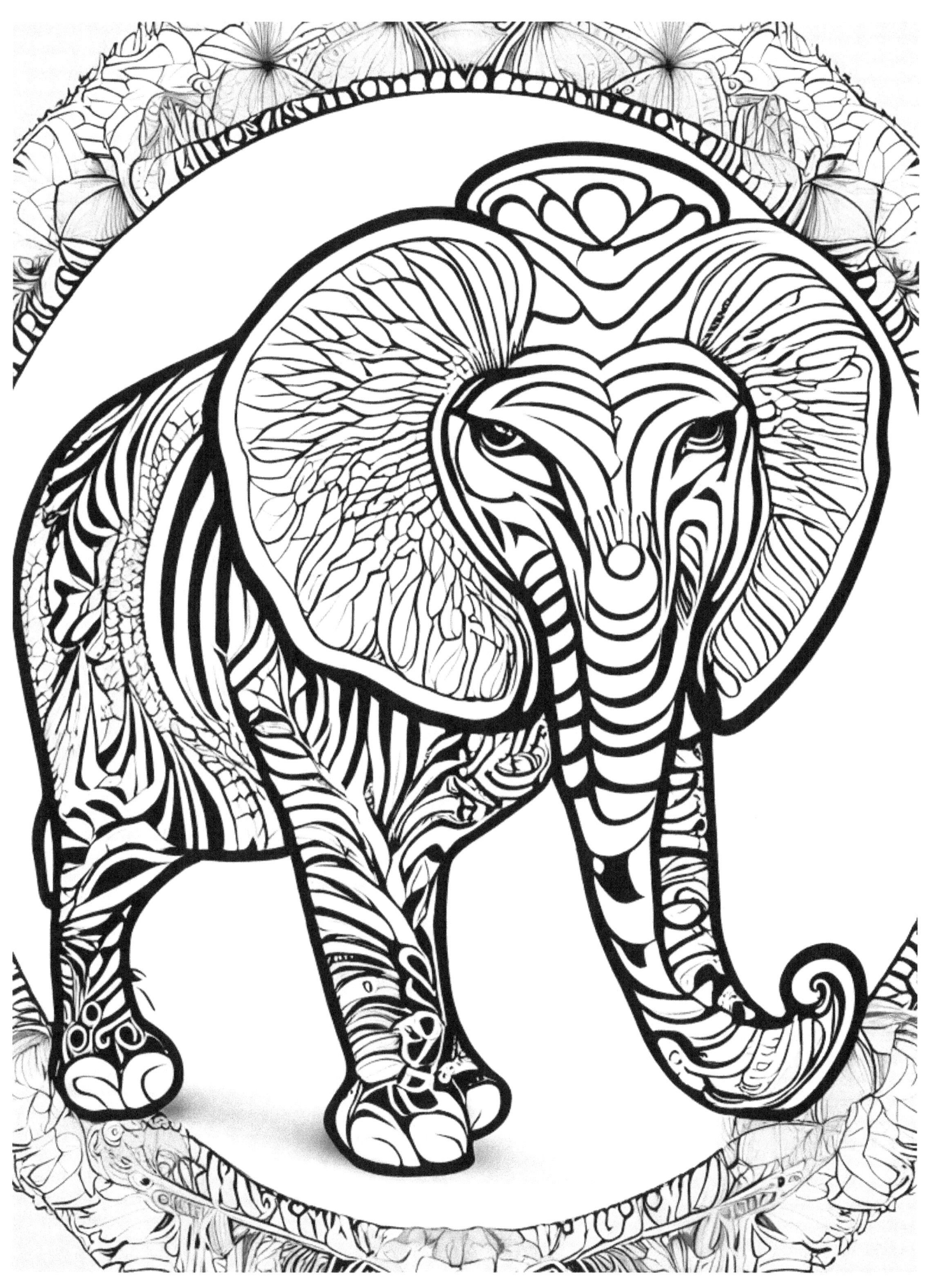

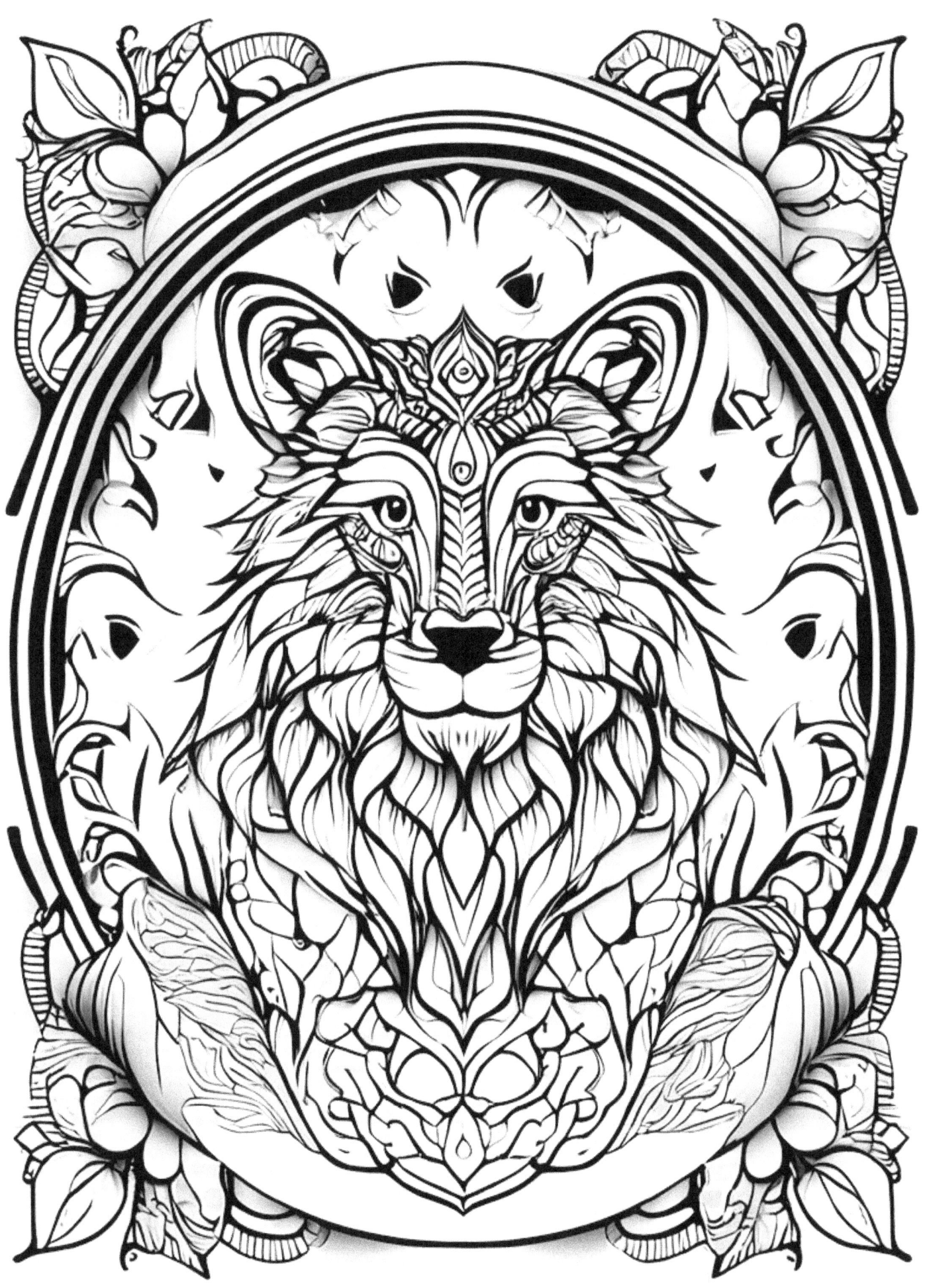

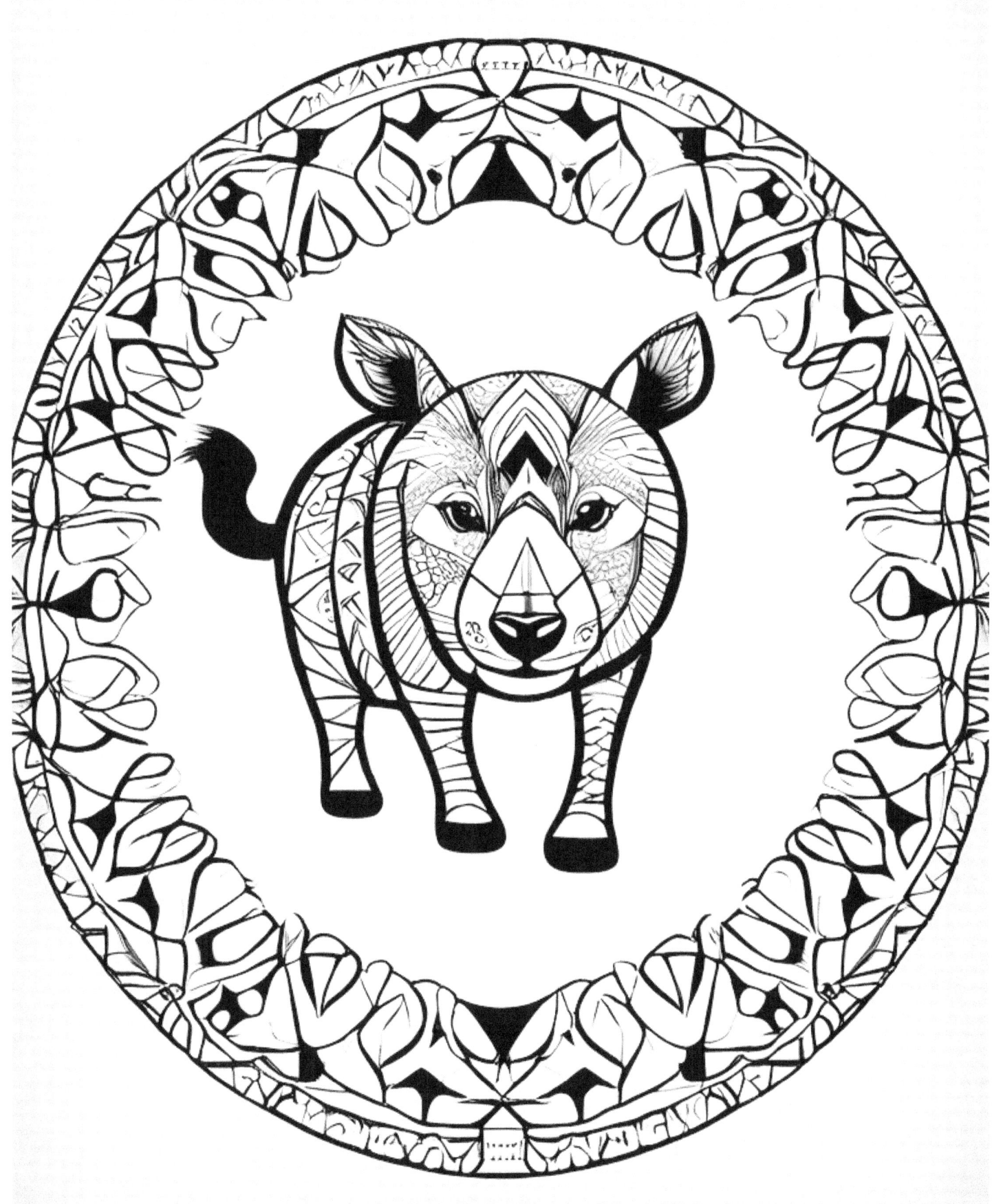

May this colorful experience continue to inspire your creativity and the serenity discovered here remain a constant reminder of the beauty that resides in every stroke of paint.

May your journey of relaxation and authenticity persist far beyond the last colorful pages.

Until the next trip through the Magic Mandalas, where magic and peace intertwine.